AN AVIATOR'S JOURNEY

TALES OF A CORPORATE PILOT

Ivan Luciani

An Aviator's Journey – Tales of a Corporate Pilot
By Ivan Luciani

Copyright © 2015 Ivan Luciani
Print Edition
CreateSpace, Charleston SC

License Notes

Thank you for purchasing this book. This book remains the copyrighted property of the author, and may not be redistributed to others for commercial purposes. If you enjoyed this book and believe that it could be of benefit to others, particularly aspiring young aviators, you have the permission of the author to share it and his appreciation for doing so.

Copyrighted Images Reprinted with Permission
Shutterstock License Agreement
Top of Descent – James Albright

Names associated with certain persons, companies, hotels, airlines, and flight training centers have been changed. Aircraft registration markings have also been changed.

Cover layout design by Joleene Naylor
Cover illustration © Shutterstock.com

ISBN-13: 978-1515305835
ISBN-10: 151530583X

DEDICATION

THIS BOOK IS DEDICATED TO my parents to whom I am forever grateful. Through great sacrifice and hardship they sent me overseas and put me through flight training and college. This incredible effort on their part set me up on the path to success. Thanks to them, those four years at Metropolitan State College of Denver have had, and will continue to have, a positive effect on an aviation career that currently spans 34 years flying around the world. It was because of their unwavering support for my chosen career, and their continuous encouragement, that I was able to pursue and eventually achieve my dream of becoming an aviator.

ACKNOWLEDGMENT

OVER THE YEARS I HAVE seen and done many things during my travels around the world. Some of these events are memorable in a way that I have found worthwhile sharing. From time to time, I have shared some of these anecdotes and experiences with my family and a few friends. My mother, who has thoroughly enjoyed listening to my stories, has repeatedly encouraged me to put them in writing in the form of a book. So here they are, Mom. These are some of the most memorable events that I have experienced so far in this wonderful career. Incidentally, writing them all down began with a little story that I wrote shortly after a mountain biking accident I suffered in October 2014. That story, "Another mountain to climb," is included in this book. After reading that particular story my dear Uncle Ignacio, who is 90 years old and an avid reader, told me, "I wish to know more about your adventures, so shoulder injury or not, keep following the path of Ernest Hemingway." Knowing that he would thoroughly enjoy reading about these "adventures" gave me the motivation to finally sit down and start writing, and for his encouragement I am grateful. Well, it has been a great ride going back down memory lane and an absolute joy reminiscing about events past.

TABLE OF CONTENTS

Dedication v
Acknowledgment vii
Introduction xi
1. "Take it, take it!" 1
2. "Ivan, you have a new student." 13
3. My path towards corporate aviation 19
4. The most important lesson of all 27
5. The start of a new adventure 33
6. Bonjour, Geneva! 39
7. Singapore, our first home in Asia 57
8. A Latin hamburger or a Nordic steak? 69
9. The Great Wall of China 75
10. A visit to Down Under 89
11. Christmas Island and a fearless crab 97
12. Moonless night over the Indian Ocean 103
13. "Fish and potatoes…and potatoes and fish" 109
14. A walk on a red carpet 117
15. Forest fires in Indonesia 123
16. The fall of a Giant 133
17. "There is problem. Need come Monday." 139
18. "Ivan, you've been admitted to Embry-Riddle!" 145
19. "Did you check the fuel for water contamination?" 153
20. A mountain between the aircraft and the airport 159
21. Special deliveries in Southeast Asia 165

22. Cannibalism, gold, and glaciers 171

23. Air Ambulance Operations 179

24. "Dad, you can accept the job." 185

25. The Twilight Zone 189

26. "Welcome home, Mr. President." 195

27. "Captain, where would you recommend we go?" 199

28. "Do you smell fumes?" 207

29. "Welcome aboard, Your Royal Highness." 215

30. Encounter with an angry ghost 221

31. "Chelsie, guess who I am going to fly?" 227

32. "Quick, quick, we can go now!" 233

33. "Guys, I think we forgot the President's bag." 237

34. "Your landing permit has been revoked." 243

35. "Did he just say what I think he said?" 253

36. "Your name Ivan?" 263

37. Goodbye, Macao! 267

38. Hello, Hong Kong! 277

39. "Ivan, you've ruined the competition!" 283

40. Global Express and Gulfstream 550 – two very different technological marvels 289

41. "Who do you work for?" 295

42. Jean's Golf Clubs 301

43. Anatomy of a bike accident 305

44. Another mountain to climb 317

45. Approaching Top of Descent point 323

About the Author 331

Connect With Ivan Luciani 332

INTRODUCTION

WELCOME TO THE FASCINATING WORLD of corporate aviation. The following pages provide a snippet of some of the things I am privileged to have seen and done during a career that currently spans over three decades of flying around the world. As you will see it has been a memorable and highly satisfying ride.

My journey in aviation began long before that first flying lesson in Denver, Colorado. I was fortunate enough to have discovered my passion for aviation as a young kid and even more fortunate to have been able to turn that childhood dream into reality. That dream, however, was nearly shattered when I found myself yelling "Take it, take it!" while in a spin during my fourth flying lesson. It was that burning passion for a career in aviation that kept the dream alive and helped me overcome the most challenging obstacle I would ever encounter. Having achieved my own dream of becoming an aviator, I have always cherished the opportunity to encourage and assist others in the pursuit of their own dreams. Such was the case when as a young, inexperienced, but highly motivated Flight Instructor, I was informed, "Ivan, you have a new student." That particular student pilot was a 64 year old retiree whose life-long dream of becoming a private pilot nearly ended when his previous Flight Instructors had all but given up on him.

The path towards becoming a professional pilot is long and littered with obstacles. For those who persevere, however, rewards await. I often tell those aspiring to become aviators, or those who are just getting started, that embarking on a career in aviation is like running a marathon. Endurance is a far more important and necessary trait to possess than speed. The race is long and it takes commitment, determination, and perseverance to reach the finish line. Crossing that finish line is a great accomplishment and earns you the privilege of joining a select group of individuals who take great pride in what they do and how they do it. The best advice I have ever offered to young aviators begins when I ask them, "Who do you work for?" Their initial response is quick, predictable, and even understandable, but unfortunately not focused in the right direction. I am certain that early on, as I began my own career, I would have provided the same answer.

Lessons learned give us the experience necessary to help prepare for, or at least cope with, the unexpected, as I recount on "Moonless night over the Indian Ocean," "Forest fires in Indonesia," "Did you check the fuel for water contamination?" and "A mountain between the aircraft and the airport." While the circumstances surrounding some of these lessons were, to a large degree, highly undesirable, they each contributed significantly towards my overall experience as a professional pilot. An important duty I now share with other experienced pilots is to pass on these lessons to the newer generations of aviators. Through this book I have the opportunity to let these young aviators know they too should pursue and can achieve their dreams. Furthermore, and just as importantly, I am able to share with them some of the wisdom I have gained over the years.

There is nothing routine about what we do. Every trip we fly is different, challenging, and unique in its own particular way. Whether it involves flying to Milan, Italy, and visiting its iconic Cathedral or flying to a remote place like Timika, Indonesia, and seeing rare and majestic equatorial glaciers. Whether it involves flying a prominent member of a European Royal family on a demanding multiple-country trip or exchanging stories about aviation with a Hollywood movie star and pilot while on an Asian tour to promote his latest blockbuster film. Whether it involves flying an arduous air ambulance (medevac) trip and, in the process, derive a great sense of satisfaction knowing you've helped another human being who was in urgent need of medical attention. Whether it involves flying to Dili and shaking hands with East Timor's first President who, like Nelson Mandela before him, had just been released from decades of imprisonment. Whether it involves seeing first-hand the marked contrast between a prosperous South Korea and a destitute North Korea or flying a former U.S. President in a much humbler version of the mighty Air Force One. Having the opportunity to experience remarkable moments such as these make for an interesting and rewarding profession.

The stories in this book present a small window into some of the most memorable events that I have had the opportunity, and privilege, to experience in my career so far. There are many other stories, of course, but I have selected those I thought worthwhile recounting. It is simply not possible to remember every detail associated with each story but I have done the best I could to accurately describe events as they happened. To assist me with this, I have relied heavily on my extensive notes from my first few years flying in Asia, relevant documents (e.g., faxes, certificates, employment contracts, e-mails, navigation charts, flight plans, etc.) and my pilot logbooks.

Whoever you are, I sincerely hope that you find the book informative and beneficial as you pursue your own career and dreams. Furthermore, I hope you will have enjoyed reading my stories as much as I have enjoyed living them, and more recently, writing about them. Thank you for taking the time to read my book. Enjoy the journey!

Ivan Luciani

1

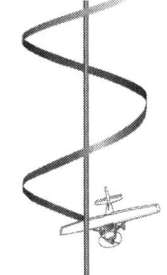

"Take it, take it!"

MY PASSION FOR AVIATION STARTED at an early age. I must have been 8 or 9 years old when my father took us to an airshow in the late 1960s at the Miranda Air Base in Caracas, Venezuela. There were a number of military aircraft on static display which we could see up close but the real treat was watching several demonstration teams performing low passes and acrobatics. One of these teams was the U.S. Air Force Thunderbirds who were, at the time, flying the twin-engine McDonnell Douglas F-4 Phantom. There were four F-4s performing acrobatic maneuvers in incredibly close formation. The number five aircraft was called the "Solo" because it performed most maneuvers by itself. From what I remember the pilot at the controls of this aircraft was someone whose callsign was "Crazy," and he certainly lived up to that nickname. The one maneuver he performed, and which I vividly remember, was when he flew his aircraft upside down at just a few feet above the runway. As he approached the end of the runway he pitched up, still upside down, as he lit up the afterburners, rapidly gaining altitude and eventually disappearing from sight. The sound was deafening and flames were coming out of the engines' exhausts. Little did my father suspect that what I had seen would one day define my life. I knew right then and there that I wanted to become an aviator and fly jets.

Fast-forward to 1981. I am living and studying in Denver, Colorado. My dream of becoming a pilot turns to reality as I enroll in the Rocky Mountain Academy's Private Pilot course after just seven months of learning English. My English was still very limited but that did not stop me from enrolling in flight training as I was eager to earn my pilot wings. In conjunction with ground school training I was assigned a Flight Instructor and we scheduled the first few flight training sessions. Flight training took place in a single-engine, two-seat Cessna 152. The Flight Instructor would spend half an hour before each lesson briefing me on that day's session and answering any question I may have had from the previous lesson. The first two or three flying lessons consisted of general familiarization with the aircraft and its components, pre-flight inspection procedures, the airport environment, the training area, traffic see-and-avoid techniques, two-way radio communication with air traffic control as well as some basic maneuvers such as straight-and-level flight, turns, climbs, and descents. During the flight the Flight Instructor would first demonstrate how a particular maneuver was performed, and then hand over the controls so that I could do it. With the engine located at the front of the aircraft, the cockpit is a very noisy environment. Although noise-canceling, voice-activated headphones were available in some of the more advanced aircraft, none of the basic training aircraft had them, so in order to communicate with each other we had to speak up very loudly. Despite being a bit nervous I was excited about the experience. I was flying and on my way to earning a Private Pilot certificate: the first step on the path of becoming a professional pilot.

When I showed up at the flight school for my fourth flying lesson, with a little less than three flight hours of dual instruction recorded in my brand new pilot's logbook, I was informed that my Flight Instructor was unavailable and that I would be flying with someone else that day. This particular Flight Instructor was a very senior and experienced pilot who also held the post of Designated Pilot Examiner for the Federal Aviation Administration (FAA). In contrast to my usual Flight Instructor, he dispensed with the pre-flight briefing and said, "Go to the aircraft and get it ready. I will see you there shortly." Little did I know this flying lesson was going to test my commitment, and resolve, to become a pilot. We took off and headed out in the general direction of the training area which is located over a sparsely populated region making it ideal for flight training. On this particular lesson the Flight Instructor wanted to introduce me to slow flight and stalls. Unfortunately he skipped the pre-flight briefing session which is the ideal time to thoroughly discuss what the lesson consists of, including explaining how to carry out the maneuvers before actually going out and attempting them. This type of briefing provides an opportunity to ask questions and for the Flight Instructor to make absolutely certain that the student pilot clearly understands what is expected. To carry out such a briefing while in flight is simply counterproductive. As previously stated, the cockpit is a very noisy environment and the student pilot is usually nervous and very busy just trying to fly the aircraft. These factors make it difficult for the student pilot to adequately process information, hence the importance of the pre-flight briefing where it can be done without the negative factors previously mentioned. In my particular case there was an additional element that added to the challenge, my still limited command of the English language.

Once we reached the training area and ensured that there was no other traffic in the vicinity the instructor proceeded to demonstrate slow flight. During this maneuver the aircraft is flown at a speed that is just above the stall speed. The idea is to teach the student pilot how the aircraft handles at such slow airspeed, the need to be gentle and smooth with the controls, and to avoid slowing to the point where the aircraft enters a stall condition. During a stall the wings stop producing sufficient lift and the aircraft stops flying. This is a highly undesirable condition which pilots are taught to avoid and, when necessary, how to recover from it. The Flight Instructor proceeded to reduce and adjust engine RPM, extend full flaps, gradually increase pitch to maintain altitude, and apply rudder input as necessary to maintain directional control. As you approach the stall speed a steady horn sounds loudly to warn the pilot of an impending stall and that any further decrease in airspeed, or increase in angle of attack, will result in a stall. The pilot then manipulates engine power as necessary to maintain altitude and speed so as to remain just above the stall speed. When done properly, the stall horn sounds continuously while the aircraft remains at the same altitude, even during turns. Unfortunately I did not understand much of what the Flight Instructor had said. It was simply too noisy in the cockpit and I felt a bit nervous. When he then transferred the flight controls over to me and said "Go ahead and try it" I simply tried to replicate what I had seen him do. I proceeded to reduce engine RPM to idle, extend full flaps, and raise the nose. I heard the stall horn, added some power, and thought that I had performed the maneuver correctly. Unfortunately, when he demonstrated the maneuver earlier, I did not see him use the rudder pedals, so I did not use them. If he said anything about the importance of using sufficient rudder control to counteract the engine's torque and, in that manner, keep the nose going straight I either did not hear him or I simply did not understand him. As a result of not using the rudder pedals correctly to compensate for the resulting yaw one of the wings entered a stall.

The next thing I remember was seeing the aircraft diving straight towards the ground while rotating very rapidly. We were in what, I later learned, is called a spin. One of the wings had stalled before the other one and this caused the rotation.

To stop the aircraft from rotating I instinctively turned the flight controls (ailerons) in the opposite direction, and to stop the aircraft from diving I pulled up on the flight controls (elevators). Absolutely nothing happened…and I was baffled. We were now spinning even faster and getting closer and closer to the ground. I vividly remember seeing farm houses, trees, roads, cows, tractors, and the occasional swimming pool filling the windscreen…and they were getting bigger and bigger. Concluding that my frantic attempts to recover from such a confusing situation had not produced any results I turned to the Flight Instructor and started yelling "Take it, take it!" To my utter surprise, and disbelief, he made no attempt to take over the flight controls and execute a recovery maneuver. In fact, he did not even flinch. His arms remained crossed in front of his chest, his unlit pipe was firmly in his mouth, and he was staring straight ahead. Realizing that he wasn't going to take over the flight controls I tried again, unsuccessfully, to stop the rotation and the dive. After a few more rotations the Flight Instructor eventually took over the flight controls, recovered from the spin, and returned the aircraft to straight-and-level flight. From that point on I was simply too shaken up to fly anymore so he flew us back to the airport and landed. I was utterly confused about what had just happened and my legs were still shaking as we returned to the flight school. As expected he did not carry out a proper post-flight debriefing either and, other than filling out the required paperwork, he simply said that on the next lesson I needed to practice slow flight and stalls again. As I drove home that day I kept wondering what had just happened. I simply did not understand it. Even worse over the next few days I started to question my suitability to become a pilot. Was this type of maneuver something pilots needed to learn and do? Did I have what it took to do this and become a pilot? Should I consider changing professions? It seemed as if my flying career was over before it had begun. I was facing a difficult and very agonizing choice: quit my dream of becoming a pilot or try to understand what had happened that day and attempt it again. I chose the latter. I was not going to quit my dream of becoming a pilot without putting up a fight.

The first thing I did was to study and learn as much as there was to know about aerodynamics, slow flight, stalls, and spins. Every book on the subject I could get my hands on, I read and re-read. Because of my limited command of the English language there were concepts I still did not fully understand so every Flight Instructor I came across I bombarded with questions. Gradually, and from an aerodynamic point of view, stalls and spins started to make sense. I learned that to recover from a spin the pilot needs to perform several actions nearly simultaneously in a coordinated and timely manner. It all begins with promptly reducing engine power to idle, if it isn't there already, and neutralizing the ailerons. This is followed immediately by positively identifying the direction of the rotation and then applying full opposite rudder to counteract it. Rudder input is held until the rotation stops and then quickly neutralized. Aileron controls, as I learned that day, have absolutely no effect in stopping the rotation. Then, you promptly "break" the stall by lowering the angle of attack below its critical point. You do that by momentarily, but briskly, pushing forward on the elevator controls. This feels completely unnatural and goes against what your intuition would tell you to do when you are in a dive heading straight down but it is exactly what you must do. Lastly, you start to gently, and continuously, pull out of the dive. If you pull up too hard you will most likely overstress the airframe by exceeding its gravity (g) load factor limits or enter a secondary stall.

Once I felt reasonably sure I understood everything there was to know about stalls and spins I scheduled my next flying lesson. It was time to face my fears head on. I was either going to succeed or fail, but I was absolutely determined to try again, and hopefully, succeed.

My usual Flight Instructor was back for my next flying lesson. After reviewing my training records and consulting the course syllabus he provided me with a good pre-flight briefing and, as he had done in previous occasions, ensured that I fully understood what was expected. We were going to practice slow flight and various types of stall entries. We took off and headed towards the training area. Once we confirmed that the area was clear of other traffic he proceeded to demonstrate the slow flight maneuver, speaking loudly but slowly as he explained and performed each action. He said, "First, reduce power slowly to idle. As the indicated airspeed decreases, increase pitch to maintain level flight. At the appropriate speed start extending flaps. Use rudder pedals as necessary to maintain directional control. When you hear the stall horn, gently increase engine RPM but not too much or you'll start accelerating. Be easy on the flight controls and make small adjustments as necessary." Then he asked, "Are you ready to try it?" I said, "Yes." Knowing exactly what to do, I performed the maneuver correctly but I must admit that hearing the stall horn caused my body to immediately tense up and my legs to start shaking. I just did not want to let the aircraft enter into an uncoordinated stall condition so I watched the airspeed indicator carefully and used rudder pedals as necessary to keep the nose going straight ahead. He went on to demonstrate stalls in various aircraft configurations and scenarios (i.e., takeoff, landing, and clean configuration stalls) which I then proceeded to perform correctly. I never inadvertently entered into a spin, which was a good thing, but I knew that to fully overcome my fears I had to come face to face with another one. That would be the moment of truth. From a theoretical point of view I thought I understood what a spin was, how it happened and, just as importantly, how to properly recover from it. I just needed to see the theory of it all put into practice. So I turned to the Flight Instructor and asked him whether he could demonstrate a spin entry and recovery. He seemed quite surprised at my request but readily agreed to show me. I started to feel a bit nervous as he smoothly reduced engine power to idle and then gradually increased pitch as the airspeed decreased. Then, with the stall warning horn blaring angrily, he applied and held enough rudder input to induce a yaw motion which increased the angle of attack on the onside's wing beyond its critical point. Almost immediately the wing dropped and we started rotating…and losing altitude rapidly. We were in a spin. This time, however, rather than fixating, frightened, on the rapidly revolving and approaching ground below I instead focused on watching him execute the recovery actions. After what seemed like a couple of rotations he recovered from the spin and returned the aircraft to straight-and-level flight. He then turned to me and, very casually, asked, "Happy?" I nodded in the affirmative while trying very hard to look as relaxed as he was…although I was anything but. My heart was still pounding faster than normal but somehow I felt immensely relieved deep inside. Since I had known what to expect the spin did not seem as frightening anymore.

We then returned to the airport, completed the post-flight debriefing, and I went home knowing that I had a good chance of successfully completing my flight training and eventually earning my pilot wings. Although that day I did not perform a spin by myself I had no doubt that someday I would be able to intentionally perform one and successfully recover from it. My passion to become a pilot had given me the strength and resolve necessary to face and overcome what would be the first, and most challenging, obstacle I would ever encounter in my aviation career.

I learned a few valuable lessons out of that frightening experience. First of all, I realized that I had to quickly and vastly improve my command of the English language, particularly aviation jargon. Second, I discovered that I possessed the determination to overcome obstacles and that I would stop at nothing to achieve my dream of becoming a pilot. Third, I learned to properly enter and recover from stalls and, eventually, even from spins. Fourth, I recognized that there was a significant difference between a good and a bad Flight Instructor. It was also painfully obvious that experience and seniority did not automatically make a good Flight Instructor. Lastly, when I became a Flight Instructor a few years later I ensured that my students understood what the flying lesson consisted of and that they knew exactly what was expected from them well before we ever left the ground. I would never allow a new student pilot to find himself accidentally in an out of control spin yelling "Take it, take it!" and have to then question whether he or she had what it took to become a pilot. As their Flight Instructor I wanted to help them achieve their dreams, not shatter them.

Although spin training is only required for Flight Instructor candidates it is highly recommended for all pilots. When spin training is carried out properly it can be highly beneficial, and even fun, for a student pilot who wishes to learn about them. As an unsuspecting student pilot with a limited command of the English language, and on barely my fourth flying lesson, that spin was a nightmare that could have derailed my dream of becoming an aviator. Fortunately for me…it did not. Despite that negative early experience I was able to continue on this wonderful journey.

2

"Ivan, you have a new student."

ONE OF THE CHALLENGES THAT every young aviator faces is logging flying hours at the beginning of their career. You are stuck in what seems like an impossible "Catch-22" situation. You don't have sufficient flight hours to be offered a job and you can't accumulate sufficient flight hours because you don't have a job. By the time you complete your flight training your logbook shows a total of about 250 flight hours. Unfortunately most companies won't consider you for a job unless you have at least 1,000 flight hours. That is why we consider reaching the first 1,000 hours to be one of the most difficult obstacles to overcome. Granted – with a total of 250 flight hours you are just learning to crawl. It takes quite a bit more flying experience to learn how to walk and even more to learn how to run. Obtaining your Commercial Pilot certificate with Instrument, Single and Multi-Engine ratings is simply a license to learn. You still have a long, long way to go.

Most young aviators are willing to fly for free, just to have the opportunity to go flying and accumulate flight hours. So what do most young aviators do to accumulate flight hours? Some choose to tow gliders, fly crop-dusting airplanes or sky divers, or become Flight Instructors. I elected to do the latter. So, after further flight training and testing, I obtained a Certified Flight Instructor (CFI) certificate and was offered a job as a part-time CFI at the Rocky Mountain Academy, a flight school located at the Jefferson County Airport, Denver, Colorado. This opportunity was given to me as part of my undergraduate studies. Foreign students like me could legally work in a related field in order to obtain practical experience for up to a year after graduation from college. That's how I was able to reach the 1,000 flight-hour milestone.

As a CFI, you are told to consider a student pilot as someone who is trying to kill you. The rationale for this is that in order for them to be able to learn, they have to be allowed to make mistakes…but only to a certain degree. If you take over the flight controls as soon as they are about to make a mistake they won't get a chance to see the outcome and learn from it. Having said that it was our responsibility as Flight Instructors to always be ready to take over the controls at a certain point in order to prevent a bad situation from getting dangerously worse. Letting a student pilot inadvertently enter into a spin was simply <u>not</u> the way to go. You want to teach them, not scare them away!

Most of my students were undergoing basic flight training to obtain a Private Pilot certificate. Others just wanted to go up for a demo or sightseeing flight. I treasured every opportunity to get in the cockpit and fly...and although I was getting paid eleven dollars an hour I would have gladly done it for free. I was young, eager, and very motivated. For me it was not a job, it was a privilege and I was grateful...and that was my state of mind when I was called into the office one day and informed, "Ivan, you have a new student." That is how I met Bob. Little did I know the next few months would test my resolve and abilities as a Flight Instructor.

Bob had just retired after working for over 30 years for the U.S. government. He was also a World War II veteran who saw action on the European front and was injured in battle. What made Bob different from my usual crop of students was the fact that he was 64 years old. He had always wanted to learn to fly and now that he was retired he had the time and the money to do so. Bob was the oldest student the school had ever had...and I was the youngest and most inexperienced Flight Instructor on the staff. I did not know it at the time but there was a reason why we were paired up.

It turns out that Bob had commenced his flight training months earlier. He had already accumulated over 40 flight hours and had not yet soloed. Every Flight Instructor in the school had already flown with Bob and given up on him. None of them thought that Bob would ever complete the course, figuring that he had proven to be too old to learn. The President of the flight school decided that there was just one last thing to do before giving up on him also: assign him to Ivan Luciani, the youngest and most inexperienced Flight Instructor, but also the most eager and motivated.

I reviewed his training file to assess his progress and figure out where to start. Most student pilots solo after receiving 10-15 hours of flight instruction. Despite having received over 40 hours of flight instruction Bob was still nowhere near ready to fly solo. It was obvious that he was starting to feel frustrated. It was then that I began to comprehend the complexity of his case and understood why I had been assigned as his Flight Instructor. I was the end of the line for him and it was with that understanding that Bob and I scheduled our first flying lesson together.

After completing a detailed pre-flight briefing and ensuring that he understood what we planned to do and how to do it, we went flying. We took off in a Cessna 172 and headed out to the training area. Once we ensured that the area was clear of other traffic I asked Bob to perform some basic maneuvers. It quickly became apparent to me why Bob had not made any progress. He was tense and really nervous. I saw him grab the flight controls so tightly that his knuckles turned a different color. Nothing I said to him while he held the flight controls registered in his head, hence the lack of progress he had displayed before. I realized that the first thing I had to do was to get him to relax. Only then would he be able to receive, process, and act upon information. During each flying lesson I had to summon all the patience I could muster, go over things very slowly and often, and continuously provide him with positive critique and encouragement.

As Bob started to make progress over the following lessons, albeit very slowly, his confidence level went up and he started to enjoy the lessons. It was then that I started to see the light at the end of the tunnel. Our first milestone was getting him to solo. Once he reached a certain degree of competence and confidence we headed out to an uncontrolled airport with very light traffic for takeoff and landing practice. It was an ideal day for a first solo but I did not tell him what my plans were. I did not want him to feel pressured and then lose his motivation if I decided that he wasn't ready. Bob handled all the takeoff and landings to a reasonable level of competence so I made the decision that day that he was ready to solo and that to do so would allow him to advance further. So after landing we taxied to the ramp and parked. I then told him that he was ready to solo and asked him to do one circuit around the traffic pattern, land, and come back to pick me up. As I was about to get off the airplane he looked at me with questioning eyes so I said, "Bob, you are ready and can do this. Enjoy it and I'll see you soon." He smiled somewhat nervously and said, "OK."

I watched him taxi out and takeoff but it was the impending landing that was on my mind. I had with me a handheld radio transmitter so I listened to him provide traffic pattern position reports and stood ready to communicate with him if necessary. I saw him come in on final approach and execute a reasonable landing. He then vacated the runway, taxied in, and came to a stop near where I was standing. I opened the door, extended my hand, firmly shook his and said, "Congratulations, Bob. That was a nice job." The smile on his face said it all. He had finally soloed and his confidence level went up twofold. From that point forward Bob's attitude and demeanor changed dramatically. He stood a bit taller, straighter, and prouder. His tone of voice was steady, relaxed, and confident. During subsequent lessons Bob was less and less tense. The more relaxed he was the more he enjoyed the training. The more he enjoyed the training the more he learned. The more he learned the more he advanced. The more he advanced the closer he got to completing the course. He still required a lot of patience and a considerably longer time than your average student pilot to learn the material but there was no doubt in my mind that he would succeed. I would be there standing next to him when he did.

Within a few more months Bob successfully completed the course, passed a checkride with an FAA Designated Pilot Examiner, and earned a Private Pilot certificate. I had not seen anyone as proud of this accomplishment as he was. It was a remarkable feat and he deserves a great deal of recognition for persevering and overcoming each and every obstacle that came his way. Bob, at 64 years old, proved beyond any doubt that it is never too late to learn, particularly to those who had given up on him. As for me I had a great sense of satisfaction having assisted someone to finally achieve their lifelong dream of becoming a pilot. Having pursued and achieved my own dream, his was a dream I could certainly relate to.

3

My path towards corporate aviation

AVIATORS ARE PASSIONATE ABOUT AVIATION. Once you get the "bug" you are addicted for life and there is no need, or desire, to search for a cure. It is that passion and addiction to become an aviator that gives you the necessary determination, perseverance, and motivation to endure, overcome, and succeed in achieving certification as a professional pilot. Those same traits help you later build up the experience level required to eventually land your first decent job. For those who embark on a career in aviation there are several possible paths. Some choose the airline path so that they can eventually sit at the controls of a large and modern passenger aircraft on intercontinental trips. Others are attracted to a career in the military so that they can fly fighter jets or bombers in combat missions while in the service of their countries. There are many others who pursue a career as corporate pilots so that they can eventually work for a prestigious company and fly around the world in the most advanced, ultra-long range business jets. Regardless of the path taken, getting there requires that you continue to display and exercise the same high level of determination, perseverance, and motivation. A good dose of luck is certainly helpful.

As a student enrolled in Metropolitan State College's Aerospace Science program (renamed Metropolitan State University in 2011), I found myself surrounded by other equally motivated and driven students with whom I shared a common goal: the pursuit of a career as an aviator. What was interesting about my classmates was the vast majority of them were absolutely determined to pursue a career in the airlines. They all aspired, and planned, to someday fly for United, Delta, or American Airlines. At the time these airlines were the biggest and best paid companies to work for. Admission to the airlines' cockpits was incredibly competitive at the time. All aspiring candidates had to have a four-year college degree in addition to the necessary pilot certificates, ratings, and experience level. A very small percentage of my classmates were enrolled in Reserve Officer Training Corps (ROTC), a college-based program for training commissioned officers for the United States Armed Forces. These were the guys who wanted to join the U.S. Navy or Air Force after graduation from various universities in order to get free flight training and a job flying different types of Naval or Air Force aircraft. As expected their military flight training was intense, demanding and, at a whopping one million dollar price tag, very expensive. In exchange for the above they had to sign a six-year commitment as military aviators. Upon completion of their commissions many of them planned to get a job with the airlines. For many years these military pilots supplied the airlines with a steady pool of well-trained, highly qualified candidates. Then there was me. I wanted to fly corporate jets, and it seemed as if I was the only one among my numerous classmates who wanted to do so. So how, and when, did I know that was what I wanted to do? It happened while I was in Aspen, Colorado, during a training flight.

In conjunction with my undergraduate studies, and in an effort to accumulate flight hours and build up experience, I was working as a part-time Flight Instructor. That's how I found myself one day providing "Mountain flying" training to a student. This type of training was conducted in the Colorado Rocky Mountains and introduced the student to the challenges of high altitude operations. The objective was for the student to understand the effect of high altitude flying on aircraft performance, mountain weather and navigation, hypoxia, and emergency procedures. After completing the required ground school, the student and I would depart Jefferson County Airport (elevation 5,673 feet) in a four-seat, single-engine Cessna 172. We would then proceed westbound over the Rocky Mountains passes to Leadville-Lake County Airport which, at an elevation of 9,927 feet, has the distinction of being North America's highest airport. Another interesting aspect of this challenging airport is that after landing pilots are given a certificate to commemorate the occasion. The second segment of the course involved departing from

Leadville-Lake airport and proceeding to the Aspen-Pitkin County Airport (7,820 feet). The third and final segment of the course involved departing from Aspen-Pitkin airport and returning to Jefferson County Airport, our home base.

It was at the Aspen-Pitkin airport, while my student and I were standing next to our humble and underpowered aircraft, that I saw the most attractive airplane I had ever seen. We watched it as it came in for a perfect landing and, after it vacated the runway, taxied to the ramp near where we were. That aircraft was the sleek-looking, high-performance, twin-engine turbofan, Learjet 35A. I was in awe of this marvelous aircraft with its pointy nose, small wings, and extended fuel tip tanks. When the cabin door opened the two pilots came out and I had a chance to see up close what corporate pilots looked like. They were both wearing dark business suits, white shirts, bright colored ties, and aviator-style sunglasses. One of them was also wearing a stainless steel Rolex GMT watch. They both looked really sharp and professional. I approached them, politely introduced myself, and asked them about their aircraft and jobs. They were both generous with their time and were happy to share their experiences with me and offer some advice. One of them told me, "We've been exactly where you are right now," meaning that early on in their careers they too had been Flight Instructors logging much-needed flight hours onto their logbooks. I knew right there and then that I wanted to be a corporate pilot and someday fly business jets.

A year later, in 1985, my classmates and I graduated with Bachelor of Science degrees in Aviation and Aerospace

Science with majors in "Professional Pilot." This excellent degree had been designed to help us prepare for a career in aviation. I remember thinking after the commencement ceremony was over, which is when we were conferred our degrees, that the ceremony ought to be called something else, rather than "commencement." After all, we had just finished four long and arduous years of study and flight training. Then I realized that graduation from college was just the start, or commencement, of what would hopefully be a thirty-five year career...or longer.

I have been a corporate pilot ever since I received my degree that day in Denver, Colorado. I returned to Venezuela in April 1986 and began the lengthy and tedious process of converting my Federal Aviation Administration (FAA) Commercial Pilot certificate to a Commercial Pilot's license issued by that country's Civil Aviation Authority (CAA). This involved sitting for numerous written examinations, undergoing psychological and medical examinations, and successfully completing checkrides in various aircraft. When that process was completed, plus the conversion of my FAA Certified Flight Instructor (CFI) certificate three months later, I was then offered a job as a Flight Instructor at one of the local flight schools. Then, in January 1987, I was fortunate enough to have been offered a Beechcraft King Air 200 First Officer position by a major oil company. There had been twenty three candidates, including me, vying for three vacancies. All the candidates I was competing with were very experienced pilots. In comparison I was the youngest and least experienced pilot but I had two things going for me. I was among the few who were bilingual (English and Spanish) and I was the only one who had a college degree. That four-year degree helped open the door for me. I was so excited to have been offered the job that I literally couldn't sleep for the following three nights. This was the opportunity I had been waiting for and, after having been previously turned down by two other oil companies for lack of experience, my first real break. The company operated a fleet of six King Air 200 aircraft in addition to a venerable DC-3. The latter had served the company for over forty years and had recently been refurbished and equipped with a pair of Pratt & Whitney, six-blade PT-6 turboprop engines. That extensive modification, at a cost of two million dollars, gave the aircraft new life and a new designation, DC-3TP (turboprop). Crewing those aircraft were twenty pilots, ten Captains and ten First Officers. It was a great company to work for in terms of salary and benefits and, just as importantly, because it provided me with a highly beneficial learning environment over the following two and a half years.

After logging 40 hours flying in the jungle and landing on dirt strips with the DC-3TP and well over 1,600 hours flying in the King Air 200, plus obtaining an FAA Airline Transport Pilot (ATP) certificate and a CAA Transport Pilot License (TPL), I was ready, and eager, to transition to turbojet aircraft. I had set my sights on a large private company, which had one of the most prestigious flight departments. I showed up one day, unannounced, at the Chief Pilot's office and, even though I did not have an appointment, he agreed to see me. There were no vacancies at the time but he graciously accepted my curriculum vitae and copies of my pilot certificates and training records. Over the following nine months, while I continued to work for the oil company, every time I had a new training certificate, or medical certificate, I would have an excuse to go back to his office briefly just so that I could tell him, "Sir, here is a copy of my latest training certificate for inclusion in my file. I also want to take this opportunity to reiterate my desire, once again, of joining your team of professionals." My dogged perseverance and determination eventually paid off. There was a sudden vacancy and I was told that he said to his assistant, "What's the name of that guy from the oil company who has been harassing me for a job over the last nine months? Call him up and ask him if he still wants a job." It was one of those phone calls you never forget. I was hired in 1989 as a First Officer and assigned to a Cessna Citation II. I had finally made the transition from turbine-driven propeller aircraft (turboprop) to turbine-driven fanjet aircraft (turbojet). This was another significant milestone in my career and I was ecstatic and even more motivated. Within a few months I was transferred to the Learjet 35A and, shortly thereafter, to the Learjet 55. Most of the trips in the Learjet 55 were to international destinations. Then, in 1990, eighteen months after I joined the company, I was promoted to Learjet 35A Captain. This was my first Command and yet another significant milestone in my career. A total of six years had elapsed since that memorable day in Aspen.

I had to wait eleven more years after earning my Command before I became the proud owner of a gold and stainless steel Rolex GMT watch, courtesy of my lovely wife Maree as a present for my 40th birthday. By the time I flew my last trip in a Learjet in 1999 I had logged nearly three thousand flight hours in this remarkable aircraft. I have never forgotten that day in Aspen for it was that particular event that led me to embark on a career as a corporate pilot. It has been quite a satisfying ride and I have never looked back since making that decision.

4

The most important lesson of all

OVER THE COURSE OF 34 years working in the challenging, demanding, but highly satisfying world of corporate aviation I have learned my share of lessons. Each one of these lessons is important and has contributed to my overall experience level. But there is one lesson in particular which I consider the most important of them all. It all started many years ago when I was a young, but very proud, Captain flying Learjet business jets for a well-known and large beverage and bottling company.

Our base of operations was La Carlota, an airport nested in the middle of the densely populated city of Caracas, Venezuela. With a field elevation of nearly 3,000 feet, a short 5,000-foot runway and mountains and buildings surrounding it, La Carlota was a very challenging airport. The aforementioned conditions placed significant aircraft performance limitations on business jets, particularly for long-range flights in which a high fuel load was required. It is because of these limitations that long-range flights were always scheduled to depart from the nearby Simon Bolivar International Airport, suitably located at sea level and with a pair of 10,000-foot runways.

At the time, I was a 29 year old Captain assigned to the sleek and very demanding Learjet 35A. The Learjet was a pilot's dream airplane because it was fast and looked and handled like a fighter jet (the first Learjet, the model 23, was based and built from a Swiss-designed fighter aircraft, the P-16). I felt absolutely privileged to fly it. I loved my job and had a great sense of pride being associated with such a great company. It had excellent salary and benefits, a great flight department with top-notch training and maintenance, a fleet of business jets, a Bell 206 helicopter, and both domestic and international flight operations. For such a young person I felt like I was already at the top of my game. Little did I know I was in for a big surprise.

One of the First Officers and I were assigned to fly a trip to Fort Lauderdale, Florida, with the sister and family of the company's President. The day before our scheduled departure we flew the aircraft to the Simon Bolivar International Airport. After landing we carried out the post-flight inspection, refueled the aircraft, completed the required paperwork, prepared and submitted the flight plan for the following day, and ordered the in-flight catering for our passengers. When these tasks were completed we rented a car and drove back to

Caracas.

Early the following morning we drove back to the airport. Once at the aircraft, we received and loaded the catering and started performing our pre-flight inspection checks in preparation for a 9 AM departure. Everything was going according to plan until my First Officer came to me and said, "Ivan, they didn't bring the catering exactly as I ordered it yesterday and there is not enough time for them to replace it before our departure." So I said, "OK, let me take a look." Instead of an assorted sandwich tray the catering that was brought to us consisted of a wide selection of pastries, butter, and different types of jams. There was also sliced fresh fruit, a cheese tray, fresh-squeezed orange juice, and coffee. Considering that the Learjet 35A does not have a galley this catering seemed suitable for an early morning flight. "OK," I said, "I will explain what happened to our passengers."

My relationship with these particular passengers had always been friendly, courteous, and respectful while still being on a first name basis. When they arrived I greeted them warmly and they reciprocated. We then spent a few minutes casually chatting about our respective kids, the weather, their trip to Fort Lauderdale, etc. Finally, I explained what had happened with the catering and offered my apologies. "Don't worry about it Ivan," they said. I then conveyed this message to my First Officer who breathed a sigh of relief.

We had an on time departure with an unrestricted climb. Within 30 minutes we reached a cruise altitude of FL390 (Flight Level of 39,000 feet) and started accelerating to a cruise speed of Mach 0.80. It was a beautiful day with clear skies and smooth air. No delays were anticipated on our arrival into Fort Lauderdale. Once we completed the Cruise checklist and our initial flight plan checks, the First Officer got out of his seat, retrieved the catering from the storage cabinets, and presented it to our passengers. When he returned to the cockpit he said, "Ivan, I don't think the passengers are happy with the catering." So I asked, "Did they say anything?" "No, they didn't," he said, "but they gave me a look." "Alright," I said, "I will talk to them about it once again after we arrive in Fort Lauderdale."

Upon an uneventful descent, approach, and landing we taxied to the U.S. Customs ramp and after going through immigration I decided to chat with the passengers. We had another casual and pleasant conversation about the kids, and their shopping and sightseeing plans. I asked them whether they had enjoyed the flight and then I offered my apologies once again for the catering incident. They seemed to be in good spirits and eager to get going so they said goodbye and left in their limo. My First Officer and I proceeded to taxi the aircraft to its overnight parking stand and then carried out post-flight inspection procedures. Once finished, we rented a car and drove to our hotel.

Within minutes of checking in and entering my hotel room my cellphone rang (those '90s cellphones were called "bricks" because of their large size and weight). It was the office. "Ivan, what happened during the flight?" asked the person on the other side of the line. I said, "I am not sure what you mean. We had an on time departure, a smooth flight, and no delays on arrival." She said, "No, something happened with the catering." I understood then what she had meant when she asked what happened "during" the flight. So I explained what happened with the catering order, what was actually delivered, my two conversations with the passengers, how they had accepted my apologies, and that they seemed OK when they left. What she said next left me absolutely flabbergasted. She said, "The President has said that the next time there is a problem with the catering the crew will be fired." Upon hearing this I had to sit down in order to process what I had just heard and try to make sense out of it. Needless to say I initially felt confused, then deeply concerned, and lastly, incredibly disappointed.

Did we almost lose our jobs because of a catering order? It certainly seemed so. It did not matter that two dedicated, highly-qualified, and experienced professional pilots had flown an advanced aircraft and its passengers on an international flight in a safe and efficient manner. It did not matter that what had happened to the catering order had been beyond our control. It did not matter that these particular passengers and I had always had what appeared to be a very friendly and courteous relationship. It did not matter that I had explained what had happened and had apologized for it. The end result was the same and the message crystal clear; we were dispensable and could be easily fired. It became evident that it wouldn't take much for the company and its President to suddenly let us go...and no one would lose any sleep over our dismissal and departure. In the end we had been allowed to keep our jobs but this was a bitter lesson to learn for a young and proud college graduate and professional pilot like myself. To suddenly realize that my financial well-being, and that of my wife and kids, could rest on a catering order was absolutely shocking. But it also opened my eyes, albeit brusquely, and taught me the most important lesson I have ever learned in my career.

I decided right there and then to pursue and achieve as much financial solvency and independence as possible. Knowing now that there was no such thing as job security and stability, even when you do your absolute best, forced me to ensure that I was always prepared financially to weather any sudden and drastic storm. Reducing and eliminating debt such as mortgage and credit card payments, while simultaneously and continuously increasing my financial safety net, became my priorities. Having zero debt and the equivalent to at least a one-year salary reserve provided me with a much needed sense of security. If I suddenly lost my job, or elected to resign for whatever reason, my family was not going to suffer. There are many things that I can't control such as the error with the catering order described earlier, or how certain passengers may respond to it, but I can certainly control the aftermath by not ever allowing anyone to shatter my family's financial and emotional well-being, even temporarily. Fortunately, I have never found myself in a situation where I had to rely on this safety net, but as the saying goes, "Hope for the best but be prepared for the worst."

I have never forgotten the lesson I learned that day and have since lived my life accordingly. Ironically, I am very grateful to the company's President for forcing me to recognize, understand, and accept how fragile a job can be and how important it is to be prepared financially in order to better handle any sudden and unexpected surprises. Despite the bitter experience I feel that this has been the most important lesson of all.

5

The start of a new adventure

MY EXPERIENCE WITH JET FAR East, subsequently renamed BizJet Services, started on a day I was casually browsing the latest issue of *Business & Commercial Aviation* magazine while sipping coffee at a business aviation terminal in Fort Lauderdale, Florida. When I reached the "Job Opportunities" section I noted with curiosity an advertisement for Learjet and Falcon 50 Captains and First Officers to be based in Singapore. After determining that I met the qualifications and experience required for the Learjet Captain position, it occurred to me that if I were to get that job my wife Maree would be a lot closer to her home in Thailand, and would be able to visit her family more often. Maree and I had gotten married in Thailand after graduating from college in the U.S. and had been living in Caracas, Venezuela, for the previous nine years.

Because of the distance, and the high cost involved, she only traveled to Thailand every two or three years. So I decided to prepare and fax a curriculum vitae knowing full well that the chances of being offered a position would be slim. I was curious to see how far I could get and figured I had nothing to lose and much to gain by scoring a few points with my dear Thai wife. After all, she had already sacrificed a lot to follow me to the other side of the planet – the least that I could do was to try. At the time Maree and our kids were in Bangkok, Thailand, spending the summer holidays with her family. When she heard about the Singapore job she was elated but I had to tell her not to get her hopes up since jobs in aviation were very competitive and that there were probably hundreds more applying for the same job. She was still pleased and very grateful about it. I had not been offered a job yet and I was doubtful that an offer would be forthcoming but, as far as she was concerned, I had shown a willingness to move to the other side of the planet for her. I had already scored a few points. Hurrah!

Ten days later I was back in Fort Lauderdale and waiting for me at the lounge's front desk was a fax. It said that they had received my curriculum vitae, that I had passed the initial screening process, and was asked to provide additional information. It also said that in response to their advertisement they had received "over 150 resumes; some of which were very impressive indeed." I was pleasantly surprised I had made it this far but later that day when I faxed the additional information requested I did not think that I would hear back from them again. A few days later I was back in

Caracas when my phone rang in the middle of the night. It was a long-distance call from Singapore. The name of the person calling was Adrian, Director of Safety for Jet Far East, and he urgently needed me to provide him a copy of my FAA medical certificate as I was being considered for a Learjet position. He explained that Jet Far East was a Swiss company that had been operating out of Singapore since 1988 and was currently flying Swiss-registered Learjet and Falcon business jets with Swiss flight crews from Jet Geneva. New pilots were being hired to replace them after obtaining their Swiss pilot certification. He went on to say that they were also planning to base a Falcon 50 business jet in Zhuhai, China. We then discussed salary and benefit details. Needless to say, I couldn't go back to sleep. Within a few hours I received another long-distance call. The caller was Brian Jones, Jet Far East's recently hired Chief Pilot, who asked whether I had received the faxes they had sent me. I said that I had received them and had just spoken to Adrian a few hours earlier. Everything was happening too fast and I started to wonder whether I had truly thought things through before sending that curriculum vitae a couple of weeks earlier. I had never actually expected it to go this far and I began to ask myself whether I would really go to Singapore should they offer me the job. The next day I met with my parents and explained to them what was happening. Their initial reaction was that of surprise. The thought of my moving to Singapore for a year or more did not really please them, but as always, they gave me their full support. The following morning my father called from his office to say that they had received a fax addressed to me. It was a formal Letter of Appointment, dated October 10, 1995, from Jet Far East accompanied by a one-year employment contract. It had really happened and I asked myself "What have I gotten myself into?" That night I called my wife and asked her, "How would you like to live in Singapore for a year?" She was absolutely delighted about the prospect so I signed and faxed the employment contract to Adrian. The following day, still pondering what I was getting myself into, I resigned from my current job and walked away from another job offer flying a Challenger 601 for a prestigious local bank. It was time to get ready to go to Singapore for the start of this new adventure, but before I could do so I learned that I would first be going to Geneva, Switzerland.

A new adventure was about to begin, but there were two things I did not know at the time. First, the one-year stay in Asia was going to be extended for many more years. Initially we extended it for just one more year – then another, and another, and another. As of this writing it has been nineteen years so far…and counting. Second, accepting that job would be one of the best decisions I have ever made. Sure, I was leaving a comfortable job, walking away from another highly attractive job offer, and taking a huge leap of faith into the unknown. It was definitely a big risk, but it couldn't have worked out better.

My lovely wife Maree now visits her family regularly and absolutely enjoys living in Asia. Our two young kids grew up learning about new cultures, customs, and languages, and in the process, became true citizens of the world. As for me, the professional experience I have gained, and the financial benefits I have received over the years, have been considerable. Remarkably, it all began with a magazine, a cup of coffee, a little curiosity…and a desire to score a few points with my soul mate.

6

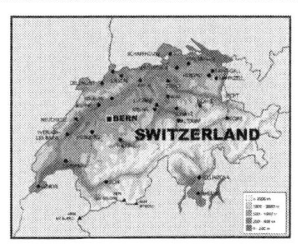

Bonjour, Geneva!

WITHIN A FEW DAYS OF signing a one-year contract with Jet Far East, I received another fax with instructions to proceed to Geneva, Switzerland, in order to undergo the Swiss pilot license certification and to complete an internal training and testing program. Soon thereafter I received a call from a travel agency advising that business class tickets were ready for collection and that I would be traveling to Geneva via Amsterdam with a major European airline. This would be the first time I had ever traveled to Europe and I found it very interesting to learn that this new Asian adventure would begin not in Asia but in the old continent. Bonjour, Geneva!

When I arrived in Geneva I met the other five recently hired pilots, including Brian Jones, Jet Far East's Chief Pilot. Our group of six consisted of two Americans, two Swedes, one Romanian, and a Venezuelan. It was a diverse and interesting group to say the least. We had been hired with the objective of eventually replacing all the Jet Geneva Swiss pilots who, at the time, were currently flying in Singapore on a rotation basis. Our first task, however, was to promptly learn how to deal with our Swiss hosts and counterparts in order to demonstrate that we were up to the task. I could already sense a bit of tension in the air as they probably felt that we were there to take jobs away from them. To a certain degree, that was true.

Jet Geneva was a well known and highly regarded Swiss company based at the Geneva airport. It had an Air Operator's Certificate (AOC) issued by the Federal Office of Civil Aviation (FOCA) and operated worldwide with a large fleet of executive business jets. These included several Learjet 35As, Falcon 50s and 900s, and Challenger 601s.

Jet Far East, our employer, was based in Singapore and had previously been a wholly owned subsidiary of Jet Geneva until one of its largest shareholders bought it. Despite the fact that it was now a separate company it still operated Swiss-registered aircraft owned by Jet Geneva, still flown by its flight crews, and operated commercially under its AOC. The new owner wanted to replace the Jet Geneva pilots, who rotated every month between Geneva and Singapore, with full-time flight crews permanently based in Singapore. That's where we came in. The plan was for the six of us to obtain Swiss pilot licenses, complete Jet Geneva's internal training and testing program, and then be authorized to operate their Singapore-based, Swiss-registered aircraft under the auspices of their AOC. To a large degree, even after we eventually replaced the Swiss pilots, Jet Far East would remain heavily dependent on Jet Geneva.

The following morning the six of us met in the lobby of the hotel for breakfast and then proceeded to the Jet Geneva office where we had an appointment with Howard Peterson, the Chief Pilot of the Learjet fleet. Howard was a young guy who came across as very professional and friendly. He welcomed us to Geneva and then explained the process we would have to complete before we would be allowed to fly their jets. We had to first of all submit for review and approval all of our current pilot's licenses, medical certificates, most recent training records, and pilot logbooks. With regards to the latter, they wanted to see pilot logbooks that had been formally stamped and endorsed on every page by the various companies we had flown for. The purpose of this unusual requirement was simply to assess whether the total flight hours shown on our logbooks were indeed accurate. Having our logbooks stamped in such a manner was not a common practice but, fortunately for me, I had had the foresight to have my most recent logbook stamped and endorsed by the last two companies I had worked for. A couple of the other guys were not so fortunate and had to sort that out. Second, we had to undergo a medical examination conducted by a FOCA Aviation Medical Examiner and successfully obtain a Swiss Class 1 medical certificate. Third, we had to become thoroughly familiar with Jet Geneva's Flight Operations Manual (FOM). Fourth, we had to pass two Air Law examinations administered by FOCA. Fifth, we had to undergo a recurrent simulator training program and, once this was completed, pass a checkride conducted by a FOCA Aviation Examiner (called "Experts" in Switzerland). Lastly, upon receipt of a Swiss FOCA pilot's license, we would then have to fly 10-15 flights with a Jet Geneva Training Captain. Provided there were no surprises the whole process would take about six weeks. A few days after the initial meeting with Howard I was informed by Brian, our own Chief Pilot that, in addition to the Learjet, I would also undergo Falcon 50 initial training. This last bit of information was like a dream come true. The Dassault Falcon 50 was a sexy-looking, super sleek, three-engine business jet. It would be a real privilege to fly one. And so the process began.

The medical examination was very similar to what you would expect anywhere else in the world and none of us had any issues obtaining a FOCA Class 1 medical certificate. There were two things about the medical examination, however, that I have not forgotten. First, the medical examiner, a very friendly guy who spoke English with a strong French accent, spoke non-stop before the examination, during the examination, and after the examination. I suspect that being non-Swiss pilots probably made us a bit of a novelty and provided him an opportunity to practice his English. The second thing I have not forgotten was the U.S. $300 fee, paid in Swiss Francs – an astronomical amount in 1996 – which was several times more than what aviation medical examinations would normally cost in most countries.

To prepare for the written examinations we were provided with all the necessary books and training material so that we could study on our own over the following days. The content of the material wasn't particularly difficult, just different. It was a matter of absorbing, understanding, and being able to recall tons of new rules, regulations, and procedures. On our second week in Geneva we enrolled in a five-day Air Law course at a local flight school. The training was conducted by a Swiss air traffic controller who was extremely professional and knowledgeable. He also looked like a member of the Hells Angels motorcycle club – he had several tattoos and a long ponytail, wore old jeans, and even rode a Harley Davidson bike! How cool is that? I enjoyed learning the material and felt that the course had served to reinforce what I had already learned on my own as well as to clarify several areas of confusion I had had. By the time we finished the course I felt like I understood the material fairly well and was eagerly looking forward to sitting for the examinations.

The examinations were administered once a month by FOCA in Zurich. This meant that if we failed any examination we would have to wait for another month before having the opportunity to retake it. Staying in Switzerland for an extra month would have been very costly and absolutely embarrassing so the pressure to pass the examinations on the first try was huge. It was explained to us that each examination had 50 multiple-choice questions, a 40-minute time limit, and a passing score of 80%. There was nothing unusual about any of this except that each incorrectly answered question would automatically invalidate a correctly answered one. In early November 1995 we drove for two hours across the beautiful Swiss countryside towards Zurich. The tension inside the van was palpable. I felt confident that I knew the material but still felt a bit nervous for myself and for my colleagues. We just couldn't afford to fail these examinations. When I finally sat for the first examination I quickly realized that some of the language used did not make sense. It turns out the examinations had been translated to English from either French or German and whoever did the translation did not seem to know English all that well. This created a problem and level of difficulty we had not anticipated. The key to this type of multiple-choice examination is to read the question, and each of the answers, carefully. There are usually two answers that can be easily identified as being incorrect and can be discarded right away. Then, it is a matter of picking the correct answer out of the two remaining choices. The problem with these FOCA examinations was that both probable choices included words in them that did not make sense. I did the best I could but it was very frustrating, to say the least. When I finished taking both examinations I felt like I had done reasonably well but wasn't entirely certain just how well. Everyone else seemed fairly certain that they had passed so when we drove back to Geneva we actually enjoyed the ride and the gorgeous scenery. Waiting for the results over the next few days was dreadful and with each passing day we felt more nervous. That first evening after the exams we decided to go out and have dinner at a Chinese restaurant down the street. The restaurant and the food were not fancy at all but, unlike most Chinese restaurants around the world, the prices were astronomical. Welcome to Geneva!

When the results arrived a few days later I learned that I

had indeed passed both examinations with scores of 86% and 87%. These scores were not nearly as good as I had aimed for, but I was still pleased to know that this portion of the pilot licensing process was completed. No information with regards to which questions I had missed was provided. That was regrettable as I was very interested to know. Unfortunately two of our colleagues, an American and a Swede, had failed at least one examination and would have to stay in Geneva for another month. As a team this was a huge setback and we felt devastated. The word came down from upper management in Singapore that they would be given one last opportunity to pass the examinations. The message was loud and clear: pass the examinations on the next attempt or pack up and go home. One of them would, indeed, be sent home.

Shortly thereafter I departed Geneva for Dallas, Texas, to attend Learjet simulator recurrent training followed by Falcon 50 simulator initial training at SimuJet International. The five-day Learjet recurrent training was uneventful and, upon its completion, Howard came to Dallas to conduct my FOCA checkride. There were no surprises with the checkride and I passed it easily. With this step of the process completed I would now be issued a FOCA Pilot's License. The following week I began the three-week Falcon 50 initial training course. As expected it was a very intense course but I thoroughly enjoyed it. There was a huge amount of information to absorb, and at times I felt as if I was drinking water from a fire hose. During training I was putting in 16-hour duty days and I often felt as if it wasn't enough. Despite the exhaustion, I felt truly fortunate to have been given the opportunity to fly the

Falcon 50. Upon completion of the course on November 25, 1995, I returned to Geneva with the expectation that I would undergo a checkride with another FOCA Aviation Examiner. When I got there, however, I was informed by Patrick, Jet Geneva's Chief Pilot and a great guy, that my Falcon 50 checkride was scheduled with a senior Jet Geneva Captain and FOCA Aviation Examiner who was already in Singapore. He handed me my newly issued FOCA Pilot's License with the Learjet rating. I noted with interest that it was marked as valid only "within the 'Jet Far East-Operation' of Jet Geneva." This was yet another indication of how dependent Jet Far East would continue to be on Jet Geneva. He also indicated that I would fly several flights in a Learjet with Howard before departing for Singapore. This would be the first time that I had ever flown in Europe and I was absolutely thrilled.

My very first trip was a flight from Geneva to Paderborn, Germany, and then to Lugano, Italy. The view of Lake Geneva and the snow-capped Swiss Alps was absolutely magnificent. The trip went very well and we scheduled our next trip. On the second trip we flew from Geneva to Milan, Italy, where we spent the day touring this beautiful city while our passengers conducted their business. We had a chance to visit the iconic and imposing Milan Cathedral before returning to Geneva later that night. After a total of five flights Howard indicated that I was now authorized to fly their Swiss-registered aircraft. With the Swiss FOCA pilot's license process now fully completed, and having earned Jet Geneva's blessing, I boarded a KLM flight a couple of days later. Destination: Singapore!

I arrived in Singapore fifty-five days after I signed the employment contract that I had received from Jet Far East. The Falcon 50 initial course had added an additional three weeks of intense work to the entire process but I was delighted to know that soon I would have the chance to fly this marvelous aircraft for the first time. Before I celebrated the completion of the Swiss Pilot Licensing process, however, I first had to undergo another checkride in the actual aircraft with another FOCA Aviation Examiner. I learned that this particular Captain was a very experienced and old school pilot. I also found out that he had a well-deserved reputation for being a difficult person to get along with. The checkride would be challenging. I would be flying alongside a pilot with whom I had never flown, in an aircraft I had never flown before, out of an airport from which I had never flown, and in a region to which I had never been. The fact that he also had a reputation for being a difficult person made it even more interesting. Other than that it would be piece of cake.

When I first met him we did not hit it off. In fact, I disliked him almost immediately and it was readily apparent that he did not like me either. He came across as arrogant, very impatient, and incredibly rude and yet he expected others to treat him with deference. I was respectful and cordial but I had absolutely no intention of kissing his ass. The next day, December 6, 1995, we would be flying together in HB-CIE, a Falcon 50, from Seletar airport in Singapore to Johor Bahru, Malaysia. It was a checkride I would never forget. Much to his disappointment, I passed.

The Johor Bahru airport, located on the southern tip on the

Malay peninsula, is an ideal airport for training and testing due to its proximity to the Seletar airport, its low traffic environment, its 12,467-foot runway, and the multiple instrument approach procedures available. Early that morning the FOCA Aviation Examiner and I met at the office where he inspected my FOCA Pilot's License, Class 1 medical certificate, passport, and other relevant documents. He found everything to be in order so he proceeded with the briefing in which he delineated his plans for that day's flight. I would be evaluated in instrument flying and approach procedures, the operation and handling of the Falcon 50, and knowledge of and adherence to Jet Geneva's Standard Operating Procedures (SOP). These SOPs were part of their FOM. He came across as professional and I had a glimpse of hope that we were going to get along. Shortly thereafter we proceeded to the aircraft and commenced the pre-flight inspection and refueling procedures, as well as the pre-departure briefing. Upon completion of these tasks we contacted ground control to request airway clearance followed by engine start and taxi clearances. As we were approaching the runway for departure the ground controller gave us a new frequency and instructed us to contact the tower controller. This is when things started to go bad. After I dialed in the new frequency on the radio he turned to me and said, rather brusquely, that it was the wrong frequency. I was certain that it was the frequency we had just been given and confirmed it on the airport diagram chart. When I stated that it was the correct frequency, as reflected on the chart, he nearly blew a gasket. He argued, loudly and rudely, that I had heard incorrectly and was wrong. He then proceeded to dial a different frequency, keyed the microphone, and said, "Seletar Tower, Hotel Bravo Charlie India Echo (HB-CIE) ready for departure, runway 03." The only response he received was an eerie and deafening silence. After waiting a few more seconds he tried again and had the same result. By now he probably realized that he had indeed heard and dialed the wrong frequency and, hopefully, that he had been very impatient and even rude to me. Trying not to sound too sarcastic I asked him, "Shall we try 118.6?" He dialed that frequency but made no attempt whatsoever to offer an apology or to say anything to lower the tension he created in the cockpit. So I said in a calm but assertive manner, "Please be a bit more patient next time." As the tower controller cleared us to enter the runway the thought occurred to me to return to the ramp. His reaction to what had been a relatively minor misunderstanding concerned me but I was also worried about causing Jet Far East further delays. I elected to continue with the checkride and to focus on flying the aircraft as best I could.

Despite the tension in the cockpit I actually enjoyed flying the Falcon 50 very much. It flew and handled absolutely beautifully. After a couple of hours of shooting multiple precision and non-precision instrument approaches, executing missed approach procedures, and entering into and exiting from holding patterns we returned to Seletar where we landed on runway 03. Seletar airport is sandwiched between two Air Force bases and its 5,000-foot runway requires a very tight and precise visual approach in order to avoid encroaching restricted airspace. Even though it was my first time landing in Seletar this was one of my best visual approaches and landings. I made the aircraft do exactly what I wanted it to do. By the time we were abeam the touchdown point on downwind, well within the airport's tight airspace, I had the aircraft fully configured (landing gear down, slats and flaps extended). Ten seconds later I commenced a descending 180 degree turn to the left while accurately maintaining the appropriate bank angle, power setting, and approach speed. I rolled out on short final and crossed the threshold at 50 feet, then gradually brought the three trust levers to idle, flared gently, and touched down exactly on the touchdown point. I then allowed the nose to come down slowly, deployed the center engine's thrust reverser, and smoothly and steadily applied brakes. Throughout the entire visual traffic pattern I had the aircraft precisely where it needed to be, and in the proper aircraft configuration and speed. The Falcon 50 was a pilot's dream airplane and I loved it. After vacating the runway we taxied to the parking stand and shut the engines down. It was then that the FOCA Aviation Examiner turned to me and sternly said, "You do not know our Standard Operating Procedures." After a brief pause he continued, "You can fly the aircraft but need to know our SOPs." Although I disagreed with his assessment of my knowledge of the SOPs I did not want to argue. I had already proven that I could fly the aircraft, and fly it well despite the tension in the cockpit and being new to it. Nonetheless, I fully intended to be even better versed in their SOPs prior to our next flight together.

Despite what had appeared to be, as I perceived it, an effort to fail me I had two things going for me. First, I was confident in my ability to fly jets, even one I had never flown before. Second, the Falcon 50 was such a well-designed and amazingly easy aircraft to fly that just about anyone could have flown it as well as, if not better than, I did that day. Even the FOCA Aviation Examiner had no choice but to grudgingly admit later on that the various approaches and, particularly the landing in Seletar, had been very well executed. I had successfully completed this challenging checkride and had added a Falcon 50 rating to my FOCA pilot's license. I was eager, ready, and now fully licensed to fly the Swiss-registered Falcon 50 and Learjet 35 aircraft and could barely wait for my first trip. I did not have to wait long.

On December 12, 1995, Brian and I received separate phone calls from a dispatcher, shortly after 2 o'clock in the morning, notifying us about an air ambulance trip to Alor Star, Malaysia, to pick up a patient and to bring him back to Singapore. At exactly 6 AM we departed from Seletar airport for the first of many air ambulance trips that I would fly over the following four years. Upon our return, our picture was taken next to HB-ZFF, a Learjet 35A, in commemoration of the first flight ever made by Jet Far East with non-Swiss pilots. A significant milestone had been accomplished and I was proud to have been part of it. Unfortunately, the celebrations would be short-lived.

The relationship between Jet Geneva and Jet Far East had been showing signs of strain for a while and a divorce appeared imminent. I flew several more trips on Swiss-registered aircraft, but within a few months the two companies would finalize their separation. Jet Far East was subsequently renamed BizJet Services and switched regulatory oversight for its flight operations from Switzerland's FOCA to the United States' Federal Aviation Administration (FAA). Significantly more training and testing would be required for each of us before we could begin operations under the FAA's Federal Aviation Regulations (FAR) Part 135. It would require a lot of work, but operating under FAA rules would offer the company considerable savings and operational flexibility compared to operating under FOCA rules. Two such cases where significant savings would be realized when operating under FAA FAR Part 135 rules would be on the renewal of our Class 1 medical certificates and pilot's licenses.

To renew our FOCA Class 1 medical certificates every six months we would have had to travel from Singapore to Switzerland as there were no authorized medical examiners outside the country. Not only was the actual cost of the medical examination astronomical but, when you added the cost of travel, lodging, and food, plus the fact that the company would have one less pilot available, it would have been a huge financial and operational burden. Unlike FOCA the FAA had several authorized medical examiners in Singapore so renewing a medical certificate was a non-event in terms of cost and time.

To renew our FOCA pilot's licenses every six months while attending simulator training at SimuJet International in Dallas, a FOCA Aviation Examiner would have had to travel from Geneva via the airlines in order to conduct the corresponding checkride. In addition to the cost of travel, lodging, and food, there would have also been a fee paid to the FOCA Aviation Examiner for services rendered. Unlike FOCA the FAA allowed approved SimuJet International's instructors to perform the role of Training Center Evaluator (TCE) so undergoing the relevant checkrides was also a non-event in terms of cost and time. The change from FOCA to FAA rules, plus the decision to have crews permanently based in Singapore, contributed towards the company making a profit for the first time since Jet Far East's inception in 1988.

I would soon be returning to Dallas to attend simulator initial training for the Bombardier Challenger 601 intercontinental business jet. I was very excited and was actually looking forward to "drinking water from a fire hose" again. Upon completion of the intensive, four-week long course I underwent another FOCA checkride but by the time the FOCA Aviation Examiner had returned to Geneva the divorce between the two companies had been finalized. As a result, the Challenger 601 type rating was never added to my FOCA Pilot's License. Unfortunately I have never had the opportunity, or the need, to use that license again.

Within days of the divorce BizJet Services and Bombardier Aerospace signed an agreement for the lease and operation of an all Bombardier fleet of U.S.-registered aircraft. In addition to a couple of Challenger 601s the company operated a Learjet 35A, a Learjet 36, a Learjet 55, and a couple of ex-Singapore Airlines Learjet 31As. These last two aircraft had been used previously by Singapore Airlines in their cadet training program to provide their 250-hour pilot cadets 40-50 flight hours of jet aircraft experience prior to assigning them to the right seat of a Boeing 747 or Airbus 340. What made these aircraft unique was that the avionics on the left side of the instrument panel resembled those found in the airline's Airbus and Boeing fleet. This design modification was intended to help the cadets as they transitioned to the larger aircraft. Incidentally, I had seen these aircraft a few years earlier at the Learjet factory in Wichita, Kansas, prior to their subsequent delivery to Singapore. They were quite a novelty because of the Singapore Airlines' paint scheme and the modified instrumentation. Even the fuel gauges were set to display fuel weight in kilograms to match how it is typically done in the airlines. It had never occurred to me, however, that someday I would fly these highly modified business jets…and do so in Asia.

Each one of us had devoted a lot of time and considerable effort to achieve Swiss pilot license certification. In addition Jet Far East, our employer, had invested a significant sum of money in the process. That time, effort, and expense was now wasted. Nonetheless, I had the opportunity to travel to Europe for the first time as well as the chance to fly Learjet business jets to a number of cities across the European continent. I loved every minute of it and was proud to have been a part of it. It was with a sense of sadness that I bid "au revoir" to what had been an enjoyable and unforgettable Swiss experience.

Years later, in 2012, I rented a convertible in Frankfurt and drove it with my lovely wife Maree to Switzerland. We then spent eight fantastic days crisscrossing the country and admiring its natural beauty. We stayed in Geneva, Montreux,

Zermatt, and Locarno. This trip gave us the opportunity to appreciate the three different regions of the country where the people speak French, German, or Italian. While in Geneva I also had the pleasure of seeing a good friend of mine from the Jet Geneva days. We've had a great friendship since my first visit to Geneva so many years ago. My wife and I love this country's natural beauty and plan to visit it again in the future.

Merci, danke, grazie Switzerland!

7

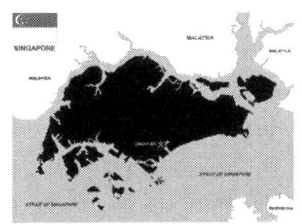

Singapore, our first home in Asia

I DID NOT KNOW A whole lot about Singapore before I landed in Changi International Airport for the first time on December 4, 1995. In those days you couldn't just google Singapore and have immediate access to a ton of information and pictures. Instead you had to rely on travel books, an encyclopedia or other people's impressions. The extent of my knowledge at the time was that Singapore was a small country located in Southeast Asia, that it had been a British colony, and that its people enjoyed a fairly high standard of living. Over the following four years my family and I would get to know and thoroughly enjoy living in this beautiful country – our first home in Asia.

Singapore is indeed a very small island country located just south of the Malay Peninsula. Despite extensive land reclamation efforts, which involve dumping soil and rocks in the sea surrounding the island, it is barely 718 square kilometers (277 square miles) in size. It became a British colony in 1824 and declared its independence in 1963. Despite its small geographical size, small population, and lack of natural resources, Singapore had successfully achieved a high level of development. Its inherent disadvantages became its biggest advantages because it forced the country to develop its most important resource: its people. The population at the time consisted of about three million citizens and was composed primarily of three ethnic groups: Chinese, Malay, and Indians. The Chinese are the majority, the Indians are the minority, and the Malays are somewhere in between. So how did three very different cultures manage to coexist in total harmony in such a small country? The answer is simple: meritocracy. How far you advanced professionally and financially did not depend on your race, religion, or who your parents were, but rather on how hard you tried to succeed. This system ensured that everyone was given the same chance to succeed, and was therefore perceived as being equal and fair to all. The end result was a society in which all races lived in harmony and considered themselves first and foremost, Singaporeans.

Singapore is among the safest and cleanest places to live. Laws are severe and strictly enforced. Possession of drugs or weapons, or committing murder, carry the death penalty…and once the sentence is passed it is carried out swiftly…by hanging. There is no appeals process so the message to would-be criminals is clear. When we first arrived we learned of a foreign teenager who had spray painted some cars and had been sentenced to caning for vandalism. There was a big uproar in the international press and in diplomatic circles, but none of that prevented the sentence. The penalty sounded cruel but the precedent dissuaded other foreign youngsters living in Singapore from breaking the law. Singapore is referred to as a "Fine city," but that title carries a double meaning. It is a fine city because of its cleanliness but also because it hands out fines for a variety of violations such as spitting, chewing gum (sales of chewing gum is banned to keep sidewalks free of gum litter), littering, smoking in non-designated areas, not flushing a public toilet, jaywalking, vandalism, and even carrying a durian in the subway (the durian fruit is known for its very strong odor that permeates everywhere and is difficult to get rid of). The government has done such a wonderful job educating its citizens that peer pressure alone is enough to deter would-be violators. In the four years that we lived there we never saw anyone breaking the law or being given a fine. I remember seeing pictures of taxi drivers featured prominently in the newspaper as recognition and commendation for returning forgotten wallets or cellphones. Similarly, a janitor would be given a prize for having the cleanest public restroom. The system encouraged people to obey the law, respect the government, and behave well toward each other. It was absolutely remarkable.

Property prices are quite high due to high demand and limited land availability. The government builds subsidized apartment complexes for low to medium income citizens, but even those are expensive. They are reserved for married couples only, and there is a long waiting list for the opportunity to buy one. Young people usually register to buy one well before they get married with the proviso that they would need to present a marriage certificate when their number is called. These subsidized apartments are built by the Housing & Development Board and are commonly referred to as HDB flats. They are comfortable and spacious without any unnecessary luxuries. Every few years, the government spends money renovating the buildings and, in doing so, the buildings are kept in premium condition and maintain their value. For those who can afford it there are also private properties available for sale. What's interesting about this is that when a new property is made available people start queuing in front of the sales office the day before its official opening. Although extremely expensive, the value of the property would continue to rise over the years making them a good investment. These properties are luxurious and have all kinds of amenities such as pools, tennis courts, gyms, large gardens, etc. Foreigners aren't allowed to rent HDB flats, so we rented and lived in private properties and paid a very high monthly rent.

Public transportation is efficient, affordable, and popular. To encourage more people to rely on public transportation, and thus minimize traffic jams and reduce pollution, car ownership is restricted and very expensive. Some of the measures implemented by the government include restricting the number of cars that can be in use in the country and limiting the service life of a new car to ten years. Furthermore, if you wish to buy and own a car, you are required to first obtain a Certificate of Entitlement (COE) via a bidding process conducted once a month. This COE essentially earns you the privilege of owning a particular car for ten years. If during a particular month 100 cars reach their ten-year service life and are scrapped, then 100 new COEs would be made available to the highest bidders. It was not unusual for the fee paid for a COE to exceed the cost of the new car.

At one point during my employment with BizJet Services, I was provided a small car. Although it was convenient to have one, especially when doing grocery shopping, I elected to return it because having a car was a taxable benefit. Sure, there were times when I missed having a car but, for the most part, public transportation was more than adequate for our needs. Incidentally, Singapore follows the British system of driving on the left side of the road. The first time I borrowed and drove a car in Singapore I managed to do a reasonable job of consistently staying on the left side of the road. It felt weird and required a lot of concentration. When I arrived at an underground parking lot I relaxed immediately and found myself suddenly driving on the wrong lane. In addition, no one told me that I had to purchase a day-pass prior to entering the Central Business District (CBD) area in downtown. This day-pass was imposed as a way to discourage drivers from entering the CBD area if they had no business to conduct there. This minimized traffic congestion in downtown. I entered the CBD area twice that day completely oblivious to this requirement. A few days later an envelope arrived at the office with two hefty traffic tickets. It wasn't difficult to figure out that they were for me. These days cars are equipped with an electronic device placed next to the windshield that automatically and conveniently deducts the fee associated with entering the CBD. This same device is used to pay tolls when entering certain highways. As long as you don't forget to top it up with sufficient funds there is little risk of getting ticketed as you pass underneath the sensors. Singapore has an excellent highway network – not only are the highways ample and well-paved, but their medians are also adorned with beautiful gardens. These gardens are meticulously and continuously maintained by an army of gardeners.

Most people speak English, or rather Singlish, Singaporean English. It is heavily accented and loaded with local slang but it is still understandable. One day an American friend of ours was having a very difficult time communicating with a taxi driver. The driver just couldn't understand what this American woman was saying so he turned around and in his heavily accented English brusquely asked her, "Can't you speak English, lah?" This three-letter word, "lah," is added at the end of every sentence as a way to place emphasis on the message or to seek agreement. Eventually communicating with Singaporeans on a daily basis became consistently easier and we actually loved their accent.

Singaporeans love to eat. In fact, I think eating out is almost like a national past time. There are hawker centers and adjacent wet markets conveniently located in most neighborhoods. The latter are places where you can buy fresh vegetables, fruit, and meat. The reason they are called wet markets is because the floors are frequently washed with water and, as a result, are always wet. The hawker centers offer varied and fairly affordable meals. It was on one of those occasions while at a hawker center having a delicious plate of chicken rice for lunch that I came across a barbershop. The owner was a friendly guy who had cut hair for the Singaporean military for thirty years. What was unusual about him was that he was missing an eye. So it was with a bit of nervousness that I sat down for a much needed haircut. I could see him using his one remaining eye to judge how close the scissors were to my ears. Fortunately, his vast experience spared me any pain. After he finished cutting my hair I saw him raise his arms in the mirror and start to pound my shoulders and back with his fists. I had no time to protest and had to endure what he later enthusiastically called a good massage, asking "Good, lah?" I did not have the heart to tell him that getting pounded on my shoulders and back with closed fists was not my idea of a good massage. I do have to admit that he did a fairly good job with my hair so a couple of weeks later I went back for another haircut. As I sat down on the chair I said, "No massage," to which he replied, "OK, no massage, lah." I was pleased again with the results so I decided to make him my regular barber. A couple of weeks later I was back for yet another haircut…but as a reminder I said "No massage, please" to which he replied again, "OK, lah, no massage, lah." When I returned again a couple of weeks later I felt like I already was a regular customer and that the "No massage" reminders were, by then, unnecessary. So I sat down and started to read the newspaper as he began to cut my hair. Everything seemed to be going well when suddenly I happened to glance in the mirror and saw what appeared to be a fist going up. Before I could utter a word, the fist landed on my shoulder and the next one landed on my back seconds later. I was suddenly out of breath and couldn't ask him to stop so I had no choice but to endure a complete beating that day. I walked away feeling sore and a little upset but learned that just because you are a regular customer and have made your preference for no massages known on more than one occasion, does not mean that the day you fail to restate your preference you won't get a beating.

The Singaporean education system is excellent but also very competitive. Kids are expected to excel in their studies in order to eventually secure one of the limited spots at the local universities. As a result, their parents place an enormous amount of pressure on them. Kids are classified into categories from the moment they enter the second grade. Each school grade has three separate sections: A, B, and C (which included classrooms labelled all the way to F, depending on the number of students in a particular year). Those who are deemed smart enough to eventually enter a university are placed in classrooms classified as section A. Those who are less likely to survive the rigors of the university but are smart enough to complete a technical program at a polytechnic school are placed in classrooms classified as section B. The rest are grouped in classrooms classified as section C and would have to settle for menial jobs with meager salaries upon graduation. Every two years the kids are reevaluated and could find themselves dropping to a lower section so the pressure on them to be reassigned to a better section is constant. The level of stress that kids endure forces some of them to consider – even commit – suicide. Unlike most expatriates, our kids attended a local school (Parish Primary) and were exposed to the Singaporean education system. We encouraged them to excel in their studies and provided whatever assistance they needed, but without over-stressing them. Classes were conducted primarily in English but there was a requirement to learn either Mandarin, Malay, or Tamil as a second language. Because our kids were foreigners and were not familiar with any of these languages, they were granted an exception. Nonetheless, we recognized the importance of learning Mandarin and enrolled them in lessons at home.

Changi airport is often ranked among the best airports in the world and it is obvious why. The passenger terminals are ample, modern, comfortable, and beautiful. They are also a shopper's paradise. Waiting at the airport for your flight to depart is actually an enjoyable experience as there are plenty of restaurants, shops, and comfortable lounges. The airport grounds look like a well-groomed park with rows of trees and colorful flowers. It is the only airport in the world where in twenty minutes or less I can get off the airplane, clear immigration, collect my luggage, go through customs, and board a taxi to go home or to a hotel. I have consistently experienced this level of efficiency at Changi but it never ceases to amaze me.

Singapore is located 1.3 degrees north of the equator so the weather is very hot and humid all year around. Most kids carry a bottle of water attached to a special strap allowing them to sling it over their shoulders, and drink from it regularly in order to replenish body fluids lost through sweat.

During the summer there are large storms which dump a lot of rain on the city and further increase the level of humidity. For the most part I wore short pants and t-shirts all the time to stay as cool as possible. I remember showering and dressing up but by the time I reached the elevator I would already be sweating. All the taxis and buses have air conditioning, as do the shopping centers, so you find that you are either freezing when indoors or sweating while standing outside at a bus stop or taxi queue.

Unlike their parents and grandparents who were born in what was, at the time, a poor country and had to sacrifice a great deal, the newer generations were born with more advantages. Although many recognize they are better off than their counterparts in neighboring countries some also tend to take for granted how easy they actually have it. I remember often hearing that the dream of every young Singaporean was to achieve the seven C: career, cash, car, credit card, cellphone, condominium, and country club membership. The newer generations are also choosing to marry much later in life and deciding to have fewer kids. This can be partly attributed to the high costs associated with buying a home, which forces them to stay with their parents for many years after reaching adulthood. Because of a decreasing population rate and its potential effect on economic growth and competitiveness, the government has been forced to open the country's doors to qualified immigrants.

The Singapore government can be credited with turning Singapore from an impoverished country into what it is today in three decades. Public service employees are paid very high salaries in order to attract and retain the most qualified and experienced individuals as well as to eliminate the possibility of corruption. As a result Singapore leads the way in terms of being among the least corrupt countries in the world. The government has excelled in having a forward-looking vision for the country and is constantly planning for the future. Whatever goal they set for the country they seem to accomplish, usually well ahead of time.

Military service is compulsory for all males over eighteen years of age. Once the required two-year service has been completed all males continue to attend an annual two-week long mandatory service period until they reach forty years of age. Singapore is surrounded by two large countries; Malaysia and Indonesia. Although relations with its neighbors are good, there has been tension in the past so a well-trained and well-equipped military is considered vital for its survival. Furthermore military service adds to an important sense of nationalism and patriotism among its citizens.

Working as an expatriate in Singapore is excellent because the remuneration packages are very competitive when compared to those for similar positions in the expatriate's home country. Income taxes in Singapore are among the lowest in the world. I used to pay about 6% income tax. This low tax environment allows companies to more easily attract talent from overseas. To cope with the high cost of housing an allowance is usually included in the expatriate's remuneration package. Other benefits often include medical coverage and annual round-trip airline tickets to the expatriate's home country for the employee, spouse, and children.

It's not possible to provide a description of Singapore without saying a few words about its most famous and influential citizen, Lee Kwan Yew, Singapore's revered first Prime Minister and father of the nation. He held the post of Prime Minister for thirty years and his role in shaping Singapore into what it is today is undeniable. Like a good father he set the example for his fellow citizens to follow and worked tirelessly to improve their lives. He was a remarkable individual because of his humility, charisma, integrity, resolve, and vision. Singaporeans are very fortunate to have had such a leader, mentor, and father.

Singapore is an excellent place to live and raise a family. It is safe, clean, modern, and friendly. My wife, two children, and I consider ourselves absolutely privileged to have had the opportunity to live there. We look back with fondness at the nearly four years that we spent there and thoroughly enjoy going back now as visitors. What amazes me the most about Singapore is how it continuously improves something that was already perfect. "Forward thinkers" is as good a term as any when describing their remarkable leaders.

We love Singapore, lah!

8

A Latin hamburger or a Nordic steak?

IN OCTOBER 1995 I SIGNED a one-year contract flying Learjet business jets for Jet Far East, a Singapore-based, Swiss company operating under the auspices of Jet Geneva's Air Operator's Certificate (AOC). I thought it would be a fantastic experience and a great opportunity for my family and I to see and do things we had never seen or done. My job consisted primarily of flying medevac trips in an aircraft fitted with a stretcher specifically designed for carrying a patient. We would depart Singapore with a medical team on board and fly to some of the most remote locations in the region, retrieve the patient, and fly back to Singapore so that he/she could receive medical attention at a world-class hospital. Most of these airports were so remote that I had never heard of them. Whenever the dispatcher would call me and say, "Captain, we have a trip to XYZ airport departing in two hours," my first question to him usually was, "In which country is that?" Eventually I flew on numerous occasions to just about every remote airport in Indonesia, Malaysia, Vietnam, Laos, Cambodia, Myanmar, India, Bangladesh, and many others. You name the place and chances are that I have been there a dozen times or more...mostly in the middle of the night. It was very challenging flying and I loved it. One such challenging trip, and probably among the first ones I flew, was to Pakistan.

It all started with a call late one night from a dispatcher informing me about a medevac trip the following day to Islamabad, Pakistan. The patient, who had just suffered a heart attack, held the post of an Ambassador of a major Asian country to Pakistan. Flying him to his country was not possible because obtaining an overflight permit to fly across China back then, even for a medevac flight, required 30 days of advance notification. So a decision was made to fly him to Singapore instead. Due to the significant distance involved, aircraft range limitations, and duty time limit considerations, the plan was to refuel in Medan, Indonesia, and again in Madras, India, and then continue to Islamabad where we would rest. Upon completion of the required rest period, we would depart Islamabad with the doctor, a nurse, the patient and his wife, land in Madras to refuel and then take advantage of strong tailwinds to continue the journey non-stop to Singapore.

We departed Seletar airport aboard HB-ZFF, a Swiss-registered Learjet 35A, on what would be a very long and challenging trip to Islamabad. The fuel stop in Medan was uneventful but the Madras stopover was anything but. The local authorities were very suspicious to see a business jet land in the middle of the night and, perhaps even more concerning to them, on its way to Pakistan. After three wars and numerous border skirmishes, diplomatic relations between the two warring countries was very delicate and tense. Complicating matters even further was the fact that the Indian Air Force had recently forced an unidentified cargo plane to land in Madras. In its cargo hold they found weapons apparently bound for the disputed region of Kashmir. Not surprisingly, our aircraft was searched thoroughly. As a result, what should have been a one and a half-hour fuel stop ended up taking well over three hours. They even asked me, "Are you carrying any weapons or have any secret compartments?" "No, we are not carrying any weapons and we do not have any secret compartments" I said. After they concluded their search of the plane I was asked to sign some documents certifying that we were, indeed, a medevac aircraft, were not carrying any weapons, and that there weren't any secret compartments on the aircraft. Only then did they allow us to continue on our journey. Before we left, however, I told them that we would be back again with a patient in less than 18 hours and hoped that our fuel stop would be more expeditious. They acknowledged the information, but were absolutely non-committal about the "expeditious" part of it. My biggest concern was that because we would be coming inbound from Pakistan, India's archenemy, an extended fuel stop would significantly delay the patient's arrival to the hospital even further.

Our arrival, stay, and departure from Islamabad were uneventful courtesy of the combined efforts of the Embassy of the Asian country in question and the Pakistani Ministry of Foreign Affairs. So, with the Ambassador, his wife, and the medical team on board our crammed Learjet 35A, we started the long journey back to Singapore. My thoughts, however, were on Madras. The delay we had incurred on our initial stop in Madras had had a snowball effect on the entire trip since we couldn't commence our mandatory 10-hour rest period until after our delayed arrival in Islamabad. As a result we were well behind schedule. We landed in Madras just as the sun was setting and the moment we opened the cabin door we were welcomed by what appeared to be millions of hungry, and very aggressive, mosquitoes. Trying to keep them out of the cabin was futile. Every time I clapped my hands I killed a bunch of them but I quickly realized that this was a losing battle and not a very effective population control method.

Fortunately the local authorities had been informed ahead of time of the impending arrival of a medevac aircraft with a seriously ill diplomat on board and on its way to Singapore. We were pleased, and relieved, to find that the local authorities graciously afforded us every courtesy and assistance they could render. With the arrival and departure formalities completed, the aircraft refueled, flight plan filed, and air traffic control clearance received, we prepared to depart with our four passengers and…about two million hungry mosquitoes. Prior to closing the cabin door we evicted as many of our undocumented and unwelcome passengers as we could but getting them all out was just not possible. I dreaded to think about us becoming their dinner during the long flight back but there wasn't much we could do about it. Flying that trip with me was a pilot from Sweden. As a Nordic man he was tall, blonde, and had very pale skin. Little did I know that Indian mosquitoes were super smart and selective when it came to their choice of blood. It turns out that despite the three and a half hour flight to Singapore they did not bite me even once. My unfortunate colleague sitting next to me, however, was not so lucky. Every square inch of exposed skin had multiple mosquito bites. In fact it seemed as if he had mosquito bites on top of other mosquito bites. It was absolutely painful to watch his white, Nordic skin covered with red swollen circles everywhere. My Latin skin, in contrast, tanned and slightly darker, did not show any signs of having been touched by our uninvited passengers.

I was grateful and surprised but couldn't understand why I had been spared the agony of being bitten mercilessly. Eventually I concluded that Indian mosquitoes were super clever and could recognize a better meal when they saw one. They probably figured why settle for a tasteless and dry Latin hamburger when there was a delicious, juicy, and tender Nordic steak available? He was certainly a magnet for these mosquitoes because nobody else in that aircraft suffered the same fate. Smart little buggers and poor tall fellow!

As for the Ambassador, he received great medical attention, recovered, and eventually returned with his wife to his country. Fortunately my Swedish friend did not contract any diseases and was able to produce enough new blood to replace every drop that had been so rudely sucked out of his body. As for the two million, well-fed Indian mosquitoes (OK, that sounds like an exaggeration, let's say there were just…one million of them) who feasted on him and found themselves transported unaware to a distant country without valid travel documents? Well, I have no idea what ever happened to them. As for me, I went on to fly to India on many more occasions…and as a precaution against mosquitoes, I either took my Swedish friend or an extra-large can of mosquito repellent!

9

The Great Wall of China

JET FAR EAST, SUBSEQUENTLY RENAMED BizJet Services, and Sunrise Tea Airlines (STA) had signed a joint venture agreement in which we would operate executive business jets in China under the auspices of STA. The idea was to combine our business aviation expertise and fleet of U.S.-registered Learjet and Challenger business jets with the airline's access to the Chinese domestic airport network. Granted, the Chinese company wanted the know-how that we could provide and would most likely terminate the joint venture the moment they felt ready to do it on their own. Access to China's domestic airports was restricted to local airlines only. That meant that the CEO of a large Fortune 500 company could arrive in Beijing or Shanghai in his company's business jet, but if he wanted to fly to any of the numerous domestic airports in order to have a business meeting with a client in a different city, he couldn't do so with his own aircraft and crews. That's where we came in. China-based, U.S.-registered business jets operated by experienced western crews with unrestricted access to domestic airports. This was a revolutionary idea, and way ahead of its time.

So in early 1996 I left Singapore for my first two-week assignment to China. On arrival in Guangzhou, headquarters of STA and our home away from home, my co-Captain and I were each provided a Certificate of Foreign Flight Crew Member License issued by the General Administration of Civil Aviation of China. These licenses were simply Chinese validations of our original pilot's licenses. In addition we were also provided STA crew ID cards, which we were told to return to STA before we departed China at the completion of each rotation. They were very strict about this requirement because the crew ID cards allowed access to certain restricted areas of the airports. The other thing that was interesting about these ID cards was that we were given Chinese written names that sounded phonetically similar to our actual names. Unfortunately I can't remember what my Chinese name looked like.

My first trip during this assignment was from the old Hong Kong Kai Tak airport to the Sanya airport located on the southern part of the island of Hainan. Our passenger was a European Government Minister. We departed Kai Tak's congested airspace at night and proceeded westbound into Chinese airspace. Our call sign was ST8012, or Sunrise Tea 8012. During the cruise portion of the flight I could hear the

Chinese air traffic controllers communicating with other pilots in Chinese. I turned to my right and saw Steve, my co-Captain, someone I had never flown with before and had only met a few weeks earlier. At that moment I felt so far away from home that I silently asked myself, "Here I am. Flying over China with someone I have never flown with and going to a place I have never been to. What on Earth am I doing so far away from home?"

My next trip originated in Guangzhou and our destination was Zhanjiang, a domestic airport. Since domestic airports were off limits to non-Chinese airlines, navigation charts were only written in Chinese. Furthermore, the air traffic controller only spoke Chinese. In order for us to fly into these airports we needed to have a Chinese navigator on board. These navigators were usually young STA First Officers with a basic command of the English language. So we spent a lot of time briefing, reviewing the navigation charts, and asking questions in preparation for the trip so as to ensure that we were all on the same page. These trips were very challenging because the navigator would communicate with the tower controller in Chinese and then translate the information. Provided that we understood what he said in his limited English we then had to process it and act on it…while the aircraft was traveling several miles a minute. Very challenging indeed. Nonetheless, the ample preparation paid off and the trip went smoothly. After landing we taxied to the ramp and, as we approached the parking stand, I noticed there were dozens of people standing right outside the terminal…and they all seemed to be staring at us. It was almost as if they were mesmerized at the sight of a UFO that had just landed. This went on for a while so I asked the navigator, "What's with those people? Why are they staring at us?" He said, "They have never seen a business jet before or non-Chinese pilots." OK, now I know what an alien feels like when he visits another planet.

One day while we were in Beijing we received a request for a very unusual trip. It was to be an air ambulance trip in which we would ferry the aircraft to Guangzhou, pick up a casket with a corpse and two family members, and fly them to Beijing. Every passenger I had ever flown before had been breathing when they boarded the aircraft. This would be the first time I would be flying someone who was not…and it felt weird. So, after discussing the dimensions of the cabin door with the dispatchers to ensure the casket would fit, we departed Beijing on what we expected to be a routine one-day trip. After landing in Guangzhou we taxied to the ramp and noted there were about a dozen people waiting for us, mostly family members. When I saw the casket I realized we were in trouble. It wasn't a traditional casket at all, but rather a very large and heavy wooden crate. There was just no way it would fit through the door. We tried several times but it was obvious that it was too wide. An idea occurred to me and I presented it to our Chinese ground handling agent so that he would translate it and explain it to the family members. We would have to turn the crate on its side as we carried it through the cabin door and, once inside the cabin, we would then turn it right side up. I watched with concern at the expression on their faces as the ground handling agent explained my idea to them. When they looked at me with piercing eyes I felt as if I had offended, not just the deceased person lying in the casket, but several generations of their ancestors. In my defense, I said, "It's the only way it will fit." They finally relented and we managed to place, and secure, the wooden crate inside the aircraft. The trip to Beijing was uneventful and, as we taxied to the ramp and approached our parking stand, we noted there were hundreds of people standing around and accompanied by dozens of official-looking cars, TV cameras, reporters, and security personnel. The first thing that went through my head was, "I wonder who is coming to Beijing later on? It must be someone very important." Little did I know they were all there to receive our passenger. There was even a carpenter who came in and, without saying a word, used a hammer to promptly remove the front portion of the crate so as to allow the body bag to be pulled out. Well, it turns out whoever prepared the crate inserted large blocks of ice to preserve the body. When the carpenter removed the front panel the water from the melted ice came rushing out and onto the carpet. This created a complete mess which we then had to clean ourselves. I never did find out who the deceased passenger was but suspect he must have been very important. Whoever he was he could now rest in peace at home.

Living in Guangzhou was tough. This was a congested and polluted city. Eating out was always a challenge, not just because of the language but also the food. I found out that people in this region eat everything, and I mean, anything that crawls, walks, swims, or flies. One evening after returning from a trip some of our Chinese aircraft maintenance technicians invited me and two other pilots out to dinner. We knew this meant eating at a local restaurant with a menu we would likely not enjoy. The first pilot promptly excused himself saying that he needed to make a long-distance phone call from his room and deeply regretted having to decline their invitation. The second pilot, realizing what was going on, thanked them for the kind invitation and offered a similarly bogus excuse. That left me to either accept their invitation and endure what I anticipated would be a dinner I would not want to eat, or come up with a phony excuse, decline, and in the process most likely offend them. If I had been smart enough I would have declined but, not wanting to hurt their feelings, I accepted. They were absolutely delighted and genuinely went out of their way to make me feel comfortable. As expected we sat down to eat at one of the nearby restaurants and they ordered a long list of local dishes. One of them happily announced that they had ordered, among other things, a "beef" dish for me. The various dishes – vegetables, chicken feet, pork, fish, and rice – started to arrive as soon as they were ready. A few minutes later the same waiter returned and placed the "beef" dish before me. I knew instantly that I was in trouble. To this date I have no idea what it was but I am absolutely certain that this so-called "beef" did not come from a cow. As I reluctantly, but politely, took a few bites into the slimy-tasting meat all I could think was, "Why didn't I say I had to make a long-distance phone call?" I lost quite a few pounds every time I stayed in China.

One morning we decided to go sightseeing at a nearby

mountain dotted with temples and many trails. The hike up the trail was steep but pleasant and the temples were impressive. As we hiked our way to the top of the mountain we came across a lot of people. It was on one of those occasions that someone approached me with a camera in his hand. I immediately assumed that he wanted me to take a picture of him and his friends. Through body language, which included lots of hand signals, I eventually realized that he wanted me to pose with his friends for the picture. I was happy to oblige, so I posed with the group and smiled. By the time we made it to the top of the mountain, and then back down, several other groups of people had asked to take pictures with us. It was a weird feeling. I guess there were not too many foreigners living in that part of China at the time so we were a novelty. Later on I learned that foreigners were known as "gweilo," which, when translated literally from Cantonese, means ghost person. With my slightly darker Latin skin I was probably seen as a tanned ghost person. My picture, and that of my colleague, likely ended up in several family photo albums in that part of China.

One early morning while in Beijing we decided to take a tour bus to The Great Wall, perhaps the most recognized Chinese landmark in the world. The bus ride at the time took about two hours due to heavy traffic and the absence of wide highways. During the ride we had the opportunity to see other parts of the city and the countryside. I had a mental picture of what The Great Wall looked like based on beautiful postcards that I had seen before which showed it during each of the four seasons. That was what I was expecting to see but when we got there we saw something that you did not see on any postcards: thousands of people. In order for us to properly enjoy The Great Wall and take some pictures we had to go as far up and away as we could. It was difficult to do so considering the number of people who were probably trying to do the same thing. The cold weather and the uneven steps added to the challenge. When we reached a point far away enough that there were fewer people around us we stopped, caught our breath, and took some great pictures. The view from The Great Wall of the surrounding steep mountains is absolutely spectacular. Construction of this impressive structure began in 204 BC and by the time it was finished it extended for more than 2,400 kilometers (1,491 miles) along the northern and northwestern border. This defensive fortification was built in an attempt to prevent nomadic people from carrying out raids of Chinese cities. Apparently it was not very effective as those resourceful nomads were able to breach it and continued, unimpeded, to wreak havoc on the cities. Another interesting bit of information about The Great Wall is that it has often been cited as being the only man-made structure visible from space. This has now been dismissed as a myth, beyond any doubt, even by China's first astronaut, Yang Liwei. Still, it is a very impressive sight and certainly worth visiting. Other sites we visited while in Beijing included the impressive Forbidden City, Tiananmen Square, and the Summer Palace.

One evening while we were in Guangzhou three colleagues and I decided to treat ourselves to a nice meal so we went out to a well-known restaurant for dinner. We ordered steamed fish, a variety of stir fried vegetables, and rice. To wash it all down we ordered a chilled bottle of white wine. Shortly after the food arrived the waiter showed up with an opened bottle of red wine. We promptly informed him that we ordered a bottle of white wine. What followed next wasn't as hilarious then as it is now. He looked at us, pointed at the bottle and in a heavily accented English said, "I have already opened this bottle." We countered by saying, "Yes, but we didn't order red wine. We ordered white wine." To which he replied, "Yes, but I already opened this bottle of red wine." Starting to feel a bit frustrated we responded, "We don't want to drink red wine. That's why we ordered white wine." He responded, "Yes, but I already opened this bottle of red wine." To make a long story short the fish and the rest of the food were absolutely delicious and we washed it all down with a bottle of…red wine.

Flying in China was challenging, complicated and to a large degree, very risky, but I found walking on a sidewalk or crossing the street even riskier. Early on I assumed that walking on a sidewalk would be reasonably safe until the day I heard horns blaring behind me. When I turned around I was horrified to find several scooters and motorcycles riding on the sidewalk! It turns out they were trying to avoid heavy traffic and pedestrians, like me, were inconveniently blocking their way. I quickly learned that they expected us to promptly step aside and let them pass. If walking on a sidewalk was dangerous, crossing a pedestrian crosswalk was absolutely frightening. Pedestrians had no crossing rights and were seen by drivers as an annoyance. No vehicle driver would ever slow down for you and yield, or even acknowledge your presence, as you bravely attempted to cross the street. As a pedestrian it was your job to avoid being hit by a car, not the other way around. Eventually I concluded that the right of way was predicated on a hierarchical system based on size starting with large trucks, then buses, cars, motorbikes and lastly, pedestrians. If walking on a sidewalk or crossing a street was frightening, riding in a taxi was undoubtedly a death-defying act. Taxis were not equipped with seat belts and you had to hang on for dear life. Drivers had one hand on the steering wheel and the other one on the horn…and both hands were used simultaneously and continuously. There was also the occasional car driving in the wrong lane and against traffic, but amazingly, taxi drivers did not blow their horns at them. There was only one way to describe it: total and complete chaos.

Pollution levels in most Chinese cities were quite high. Not only was the sky gray and hazy but you could smell and feel the polluted air. After I returned to Singapore following another two-week assignment, I felt sick with symptoms that appeared similar to that of someone having a cold. I had a very dry cough and, at times, was coughing continuously and uncontrollably. There were episodes in the middle of the night in which I coughed so much and for so long that I was momentarily out of air and was unable to breathe. This scared me so much that I went to see a doctor the following morning and was prescribed some medication. I followed the doctor's instructions to the letter and completed taking all the medication exactly as prescribed but after about seven days the dry cough had not abated. So I returned to the same doctor and complained that the medication only had moderate effect on eliminating the coughing. She examined me again, prescribed stronger medication, and sent me home. Again, I followed her instructions to the letter, took the stronger medication as prescribed, but only felt some minor relief. I was still coughing the same dry cough so I returned to the same doctor for a third time. Again, she examined me and prescribed yet stronger medication. Within a few days I started to recover and was feeling much better but suspected that this had not been a common cold at all. Instead I believe that while I was in China I had breathed air filled with silt and other pollutants that probably left my lungs coated with a thick layer of this nasty stuff. The constant coughing must have been an attempt by my body desperately trying to rid itself of it. That would explain why the medication I had taken had had limited effect, if any. It turns out I wasn't the only one of us who had experienced this.

In the cities and towns we visited we saw things that couldn't possibly be described in words. You just had to be there and see them for yourself. Because China was so different from what we were used to at the time, the company had a two week rotation system so that we would each spend only two weeks at a time in China, and return to stay with our families for the following two weeks in Singapore. It was definitely very different. I remember seeing airline pilots going to work riding bicycles. There were relatively few cars as most people used bicycles and scooters. On a return flight to Singapore on a brand new Boeing 757 from Sunset Tea

Airlines I was horrified to see some passengers clearing their throats and spitting on the floor behind the seats. Even more horrifying, no one else seemed to mind!

Today, China has changed dramatically. Many of its people now enjoy a much higher quality of life and have plenty of disposable income to travel overseas. China's economy has been growing steadily for years and is expected to eventually become the largest economy in the world. Nonetheless it can still be a challenging environment for some foreigners to live in. Having said that, my own time and experiences in China are memorable in a special way and will remain absolutely unforgettable. People were very friendly and hospitable towards us…unless of course we happened to be crossing the street!

Flying in China in those early days was a real adventure, albeit a high risk one. Relying on navigators to communicate with the air traffic controllers and using navigation charts in Chinese presented considerable challenges. Adding even more complexity to an already complex situation was China's use of the metric system (i.e., for altitudes, visibility and wind speed reports) and QFE altimeter settings, a setting that would have the altimeter read zero when on the ground instead of the more traditional reading above sea level. This system was particularly challenging at high elevation airports because our altimeters could not be set to QFE with a field elevation greater than 1,500 feet above Mean Sea Level (MSL). In a certain way we were pioneers who loved the challenge but who were keenly aware of the risks involved.

Like everything else in China, business aviation has grown

exponentially over the past decade and is now a thriving industry. The number and type of business jets commonly found today in China is nothing short of remarkable. Back in 1996 China's business aviation industry was at a pioneering stage. There were just a handful of small cabin size business jets (Learjet 60s and Hawker 800s). Today their number is in the hundreds and most are large cabin size, ultra-long range business jets. The use of business jets is now widely accepted as a productivity tool that allows business executives to conduct more business in less time. Long gone are the days when an overflight permit required 30 days advance notice. Permits today can be obtained in as little as 24 hours. I fondly remember having the privilege (and luck of the draw) of flying to China on the first permanently-based, foreign-registered business jet – a Challenger 601-1A. It was a historical occasion that, although significant at the time, belongs to a very different era.

Those of us who were there during that important early period can rightfully and proudly say that we contributed towards the introduction and development of business aviation. Furthermore, we learned about another culture and made a lot of friends. This was, without a doubt, a remarkable and valuable experience.

Xie xie (thank you), China!

10

A visit to Down Under

In 1996 BizJet Services and the Royal Peak Hotel and Casino signed a one-month contract for the lease of one of our Challenger 601 business jets. Under the terms of the contract a fully crewed aircraft would be available to provide air transportation services for some of their most important clients. Royal Casino is located in Melbourne and was, at the time, the largest casino in Australia. They owned and operated a Gulfstream IV but, due to increased demand, they needed extra capacity. As a recently licensed Challenger 601 pilot I would have the opportunity to participate in these trips and, in the process, fly my first trip ever to this beautiful and far away country.

The casino's strategy of using business aircraft was absolutely brilliant and quite profitable. It was oriented towards very wealthy foreigners who enjoyed gambling – high-rollers. The casino would extend an invitation to a millionaire to come to Melbourne to visit the casino, all expenses paid. That included having a private jet pick them up wherever they lived and whenever they wanted, fly them to Melbourne in luxurious comfort and style, pick them up at the airport with a stretch limousine, provide them a luxurious villa with a dedicated butler and a chef, allow them to try their luck in a private and luxurious game room in the casino, and fly them back home in the same business jet whenever they wanted to leave. To top it all off they could bring any friends they wanted and they too would be extended the same benefits. All they had to do in return was to deposit a specific sum of money – several million dollars – in advance at the casino…and have a good time at the gaming tables. Most of these millionaires were from Indonesia and the casino really knew how to make them feel special. So much so that the millionaires themselves would then tell their millionaire friends about the exclusive invitation they had received from the Australian casino and that they too could come along aboard the private jet. Many of their friends did join them on these trips and were in turn extended similar invitations in the future. Although the odds strongly favored the house it could also go the other way. For the most part, however, this strategy allowed the casino to make several million dollars in revenue in just a few days.

Thus we departed Seletar airport aboard N215GA, a Challenger 601-3R. Our destination was Jakarta, Indonesia's capital where we would pick up a high-roller accompanied by a couple of friends, and fly them to Melbourne. After landing at Halim International Airport we proceeded to the ramp, shut the engines down, refueled and prepared the aircraft for its first trip south of the equator. Our passengers arrived on time and boarded the aircraft. Once airborne, our Flight Attendant provided them with five-star in-flight service. The casino was very specific: only the best of everything would be served and no expense would be spared. So over the next seven hours our passengers were pampered in luxurious comfort and privacy. Nothing but the most expensive champagne, wine, liquor, caviar, cheeses, bird's nest, abalone, lobster, shark fin soup, and other delicacies were served.

We had an on time departure from Halim and a very pleasant trip to Melbourne. After landing we taxied to the designated parking stand and, as we shut the engines down, a stretch black limousine pulled over by the aircraft and stood ready for our passengers. Customs and immigration officials boarded the aircraft and all arrival procedures were promptly completed inside the privacy of the aircraft. With all formalities completed in just a few minutes, our passengers thanked us for the pleasant trip, disembarked, and then boarded the limousine for the short ride to their luxurious villa.

As I stood by the aircraft, I remember feeling that I was as far away from everything as I had ever been. In fact I felt so far away that, with a grin on my face, I said to myself, "This is where the wind turns around because it can't go any further." Once we completed the post-flight inspection we were picked up by a not-so-stretched and certainly not-so-luxurious van. Nonetheless, it was still very comfortable and that's all that really mattered. It had been a long day for us so we were ready for a shower and a warm bed. We stayed at the Royal Hotel which is conveniently located in the middle of the city. The following morning we were given a tour of the casino, including a rare glance at the private game rooms reserved for the "high-rollers." We did not get a chance to see the villas but when I asked whether the hotel suites would serve the same purpose I was told that they weren't nearly luxurious enough for this type of clientele. The casino itself did not seem all that grand, especially when compared to those in Las Vegas, but construction of a new hotel and casino was in progress next door. Business was evidently booming because they were also purchasing a second Gulfstream IV.

Over the next couple of days we went around this beautiful city visiting some of the most popular spots. I particularly liked the river walk area with its many restaurants and shops. The climate was very pleasant and the skies were clear and very blue. The people seemed very down to earth, were extremely friendly, and spoke with a distinctive accent. They also used slang such as "G'day, mate," "Ta," and "Avro." The last two were regularly used in lieu of "Thanks" and "Afternoon." The combination of the accent and the slang made it sound almost like something other than English. Over the next four weeks I would return to this modern and pleasant city several times. Unfortunately we never had a chance to see kangaroos as we would have had to drive for nearly two hours out of town in order to reach their natural habitat. We needed to be ready on short notice in case our passengers decided that they had already lost too much money or wanted to go home.

Upon our return to Jakarta our passengers would always convey their appreciation verbally and with a substantial tip. I wasn't quite sure if the latter was an indication that they had won big at the tables or that they were simply very generous. In any case, it was the first time that I had ever received a tip. My crew and I considered ourselves well-paid professionals so it felt strange to accept a tip but turning it down might have been perceived as an offense. In any case, and considering that it did not violate company policy, I wasn't going to complain too loudly about it…and neither did the rest of the crew.

I had made the first of many trips to Down Under. Over the following years I would have the chance to visit Perth, Sydney, Cairns, Darwin, the Gold Coast, Port Hedland, Hayman Island, and other cities. Every city I visited had its own unique charm and attractions but with the same easy going style. Perth, one of my favorite places, is a beautiful city on the western coast with a very relaxed atmosphere. Lots of sunshine, parks, and beautiful beaches, but the one thing that surprised me the most the first time I went there was that all the shops closed sharply at 5 PM. I just couldn't understand why. Eventually I concluded that this was a conspiracy undertaken by the government in which shops were closed early so that people were obliged to go home early and…procreate. In this manner they would be contributing to producing more future tax-paying citizens. After all, Australia is a very large country with a very small population – more citizens would result in a larger tax base and greater tax revenue to provide security, services, and infrastructure. Of course this wasn't the reason the shops closed early at all but I thought that it was kind of funny to think this way. It probably had more to do with stringent labor laws than with any conspiracy theory.

Sydney is a modern city on the Eastern Coast blessed with a beautiful harbor and surrounded by gorgeous mountains...and, of course, it is where the iconic Sydney Opera House is located. There are lots of restaurants, shops, and cafes but it is also one of the most expensive cities in the world. Cairns and Darwin are much smaller cities with their own unique geographic characteristics and history. One of my favorite restaurants in Darwin is Hogs Breath, which is famous for its prime ribs. The juicy meat undergoes a 24-hour preparation period in which it is tenderized so when you eat it you can practically cut it with a fork. It is absolutely delicious! The Gold Coast, and surrounding area in eastern Australia, reminded me of Miami Beach with its many miles of white sandy beaches and party atmosphere.

In the beach town of Surfers Paradise I saw two beautiful bikini-clad girls walking around in the entertainment and tourism area inserting coins in parking meters that were about to reach their time limit. These girls are known as Surfers Paradise Meter Maids. Inserting coins in the meters was done in an act of defiance against parking tickets as well as to promote the area and preserve goodwill. These girls also posed for pictures with passersby in exchange for donations. I don't drive or own a car in Australia and will most likely never get a parking ticket during my visits but I know how painful it is to get one. So I gladly posed for a picture with these two beautiful girls and then gave them the corresponding donation…all in the name of keeping some poor bastard from getting a parking ticket, of course.

Australia is indeed a beautiful and friendly country. It is also enormous. When you've had the chance to fly from coast to coast you realize just how expansive this country really is. I love spending time "Down Under" and have made quite a few Australian friends over the years. Unfortunately, and despite my many visits so far, I have yet to see any kangaroos!

The next one is my shout, mates! (next round of drinks)

11

Christmas Island and a fearless crab

ONE OF THE THINGS I love the most about my job is the opportunity to visit different places, some of which are highly unusual. One such place is a little island in the Indian Ocean located 250 kilometers (155 miles) south of the island of Java, Indonesia. It's called Christmas Island and it derives its unique name from being discovered on a Christmas day by a passing British sailor. Despite the fact that it is geographically closer to Indonesia, the island is actually a part of Australia. Of course I did not know this interesting little island even existed until we received a charter request from the Red Crab Resort and Casino.

Christmas Island's economy had depended for many years on phosphate mining. During World War II the Japanese invaded Christmas Island as part of their frantic search for natural resources in the region. By the late 1990s, the mines were depleted and were subsequently closed down. To provide a new source of income for the two thousand inhabitants, the Australian government permitted the opening of a resort and casino. With the island's close proximity to Indonesia, the resort and casino was particularly attractive to tourists and high rollers from that country. We departed for Christmas Island from Seletar airport one day in N215GA, a Challenger 601-3R, with a small group of very wealthy Indonesian high rollers. The one hour and forty minute flight was very pleasant, and our Flight Attendant ensured that our passengers received five-star pampering during that time. We executed a non-precision approach that, in simple terms, is an instrument approach without any vertical guidance, unlike the better known Instrument Landing System (ILS) which has both lateral and vertical guidance. We landed on what was a rather rough runway. The nighttime approach was uneventful but the strong crosswind resulted in a rough landing which bruised my ego a little bit. Later on I found out that the approach and landing into Christmas Island was considered very difficult because the island rises abruptly almost 1,000 feet from sea level into what is, in essence, a plateau. The easterly wind flows over the sea and then rapidly up the cliff. This creates an area of turbulence during the approach and blustery crosswinds during the landing. After exiting the runway, and with my bruised ego still thinking about that awful landing, we taxied to the parking stand, shut the engines down, and allowed our passengers to disembark. These high rollers were considered a bloodline for the local population because they gambled millions of dollars away in just a few days. For that, they were welcomed and treated like royalty.

The following morning our ground handling agent picked us up at the hotel and took us for a guided tour of the island. The island has a surface of 135 square kilometers (52 square miles) and more than half of that is considered a national park. Because it is so remote, and its population so small, its flora and fauna have been largely undisturbed. Perhaps the biggest natural attraction is the existence of millions of huge land crabs that inhabit the island. These red crabs are enormous and, during the annual breeding migration, move together in huge numbers giving the appearance of a huge red river flowing noisily down to the sea. It's quite a sight. These crabs are considered a protected species and only the locals are allowed to eat them. According to our ground handling agent, they are absolutely delicious. I am not a fan of crab meat so I would have never consider eating them for either lunch or dinner.

Later that evening, my crew and I had a pleasant and relaxed dinner (no crabs!) at our hotel, the Red Crab Resort and Casino. This beautiful hotel consisted of a main building, where the restaurant is located, and several villas scattered around a large garden. The villas and the main building are connected via paved walkways. As my co-Captain and I were walking back to our respective villas later that evening we came across a huge red crab standing in the middle of one of those walkways. Feeling a little curious to see one of them up close we decided to check it out. Amazingly, no matter how close we got to it, it did not move an inch. It was obvious that this crab was not intimidated by a couple of guys who were standing very close to it. We must have been less than two feet away from it when suddenly the lights went out and we found ourselves in complete darkness and in close proximity with the enormous crab. Well, we both almost simultaneously panicked, yelled profanities, and jumped backwards. As we did that, I remember thinking, "How did it do that?" meaning, how did this crab turn off the lights? While the blackout lasted I kept waiting for the crab to get even with us and use its huge claws to teach a couple of morons a well-deserved lesson. When the lights came back on a few seconds later we noted with relief that the crab had not moved an inch and was still staring intently at us. That was enough of a standoff for my taste. It was definitely time for us to leave it alone. Because it obviously did not fear us, nor did it intend to move, the two of us elected to cautiously walk around it…at a safe distance!

After a couple of days enjoying the island's relaxed atmosphere it was time to return to Singapore. The trip had been a success for everyone. The local economy had received a much needed influx of revenue, our high roller passengers enjoyed the royal treatment and trying their luck at the gaming tables, and a fearless red crab earned bragging rights for standing up to a couple of curious but likely very annoying tourists. Unfortunately I never had another opportunity to return and visit this isolated little island and its peculiar land crabs. There is something very pleasant about this place and I can understand why its native population would be reluctant to immigrate to Australia, its "slightly" larger sister island to the south. Lastly, because the island is so remote, I have always wondered whether I was the first Venezuelan national to have ever been there. If someday I find out and it turns out that I was indeed the first Venezuelan person to visit it, I will have earned the right to rename it Isla Navidad.

Goodbye, Christmas Island!

12

Moonless night over the Indian Ocean

M*y very first trip to* the Maldives was an air ambulance flight and was unforgettable for two very different reasons, one of which gave me quite a scare. The Maldives is made up of an island chain of nearly 2,000 small coral islands grouped into clusters of atolls. Located southwest of India in the Northern Indian Ocean, it is a popular tourist destination due to its beautiful beaches and excellent scuba diving. Because of the considerable distance from Singapore we planned two fuel stops: Medan in Indonesia and Colombo in Sri Lanka. Once we arrived in Malé, the capital of the Maldives, we would rest for 10 hours before commencing the return trip.

Landing and refueling in Medan was uneventful and we

were airborne again within 45 minutes. We then embarked on the three and a half hour trip across the Bay of Bengal to Colombo, the capital of Sri Lanka. It was past midnight when we finally landed in Colombo. Airport security was very tight due to fighting between the government and rebels of the Liberation Tigers of Tamil Ealam (LTTE). The LTTE was seeking to create a separate nation for the Tamil minority in the northern and eastern corners of the island. Fortunately Colombo is located in the southernmost part of the island so we were far away from the troubled areas (a year later the rebels conducted a daring suicide mission at the airport and destroyed several commercial aircraft). Once all the arrival/departure formalities were completed, and the aircraft refueled, we departed for the one hour trip to Malé. This was to be the most challenging portion of the trip because we had been on duty for many hours, had performed two landings already, and were beginning to feel a bit tired. There were numerous thunderstorms in the area that we avoided by circumnavigating them. It was also a moonless night over the ocean, which gave the feeling of being in a black hole. Looking out the window for any visual references in pitch darkness is futile and dangerous, as I found out later. Descending through 5,000 feet I turned my attention away from the flight instruments to look out the window hoping to see the lights of the town or airport. What happened next was the weirdest and scariest feeling imaginable, vertigo. I had learned about vertigo years earlier, but I had never experienced it. With no horizon visible, nor any other visual cues, I immediately felt completely disoriented. I did not really know whether I was right side up, upside down or turning in a steep bank, although I felt as if it was the latter. Vertigo, also referred to as Spatial Disorientation, is simply a mismatch between the pilot's perception of direction and the reality. With the lack of a visual reference, such as the natural horizon, my correct sense of up or down was lost.

I quickly glanced back down at the flight instruments and repeatedly reminded myself to trust them, even though my senses made me feel as if I was turning with a 60 degree bank angle. In other words, what I felt and what my flight instruments indicated contradicted each other, and I had to fight the urge to believe my senses. Instead I had to trust, and follow, my flight instruments. The autopilot had been engaged the whole time and the flight instruments indicated that the wings were perfectly level. My First Officer, sitting next to me, had not shown any signs of alarm so I knew my inner senses were giving me erroneous information. After focusing intently on the flight instruments the vertigo sensation gradually disappeared and I felt an enormous sense of relief. I did not dare look out the window until we were positively established on the Instrument Landing System (ILS), which provides lateral and vertical guidance to the runway. As we were descending on the ILS the approach and runway lights came clearly, and brightly, into view. Adding to the challenge, however, was a strong crosswind which meant that we were looking at the runway at an angle. That made the landing more difficult.

Once at the parking stand, we shut the engines down, opened the main cabin door, stepped outside the aircraft, and breathed in the humid and salty air. It had been a long trip but we still had a ways to go before getting to a nice bed. The local ground handling agent greeted us warmly and asked me, "Are you from Venezuela?," to which I answered, "Yes, I am." He then said, "Oh, Venezuelan women, the most beautiful women in the world." Quite a few Venezuelan women had won the Miss Universe and Miss World beauty pageants over the years but it was still amusing to learn that even in this remote little island situated in the Indian Ocean, the beauty of Venezuelan women was well known. What he said next surprised me even more. He said, "There is a speed boat ready to take you to your hotel." Boat? What boat? Nobody had said anything to me about getting on a boat. Well, it turns out that our hotel was located on one of the nearby islands (seaplanes are used to reach the most distant islands when transporting tourists). So, after riding in a speed boat and being sprayed with sea water for nearly 40 minutes in pitch darkness, we finally arrived at our hotel. It had been a long, challenging, and exhausting journey. Over 12 hours of duty across three time zones, three landings, three countries, including one in the middle of a civil war, numerous thunderstorms, one frightening episode of in-flight vertigo, nighttime approach and landing with a strong crosswind on a runway surrounded by water and, to top it all off, an unexpected ride in a speed boat on a moonless night. All of that within the maximum allowable 14-hour duty period. As a well-deserved reward for our efforts we were each provided with a soft bed and the opportunity for much-needed sleep. I passed out as soon as my head touched the pillow.

After that well-deserved and much-needed rest plus a hearty breakfast we hopped back on the speed boat for the return trip to the airport. It was then that I realized how beautiful this place really was. We were in paradise. Turquoise colored water and calm seas, white sandy beaches, beautiful clear skies, and a pleasant temperature made this a joyful paradise destination for its visitors...except for our unfortunate patient. She was a young Japanese woman who had been scuba diving with her husband at a depth of 10 meters (33 feet) when her oxygen tank ran out. She panicked and started to swallow sea water. Fortunately her husband was nearby and quickly brought her up to the surface although by then she was unconscious. Even more fortunately, a passing boat saw them and picked them up. The boat crew promptly performed CPR and revived her while they rushed her to the local hospital. She regained consciousness and started to recover but the subsequent treatment that her lung infection required was beyond the local hospital's capabilities, hence the need to evacuate her.

With the patient and her husband, plus the medical team on board, we departed Malé. As we started climbing and I saw the airport below I realized that we had landed in the middle of the night with a strong crosswind on what resembled a very long but narrow aircraft carrier. The runway extended from a narrow section of the atoll with a lagoon on one side and the ocean on the other. It was absolutely gorgeous from the air. Our first fuel stop was in Colombo and the trip over was uneventful. As we were refueling the patient's husband got off the aircraft with camera in hand and started taking pictures. There was not really that much to see from the ramp where we were but that did not stop him from snapping dozens of pictures of our surroundings, including some of his poor wife strapped to the stretcher. I guess he figured there was no sense in putting their photo-taking enthusiasm on hold just because his wife couldn't pose for any pictures or there wasn't a white sandy beach with palm trees around.

Two and a half hours after departing Colombo we determined that the tailwinds were strong enough to allow us to continue non-stop to Singapore, avoiding the need for a fuel stop in Medan. This saved us about two hours and resulted in our patient being taken to a top-notch hospital and receiving the medical care she needed a lot sooner. Eventually she recovered fully and returned to Japan where her near death story, supported by her husband's pictures of her on a stretcher, was probably shared with family and friends. As for me, knowing that I had helped another human being gave me a great sense of satisfaction. It had been a long, challenging, and exhausting trip and we completed it safely. That was a great feeling and it just doesn't get any better than that. I have never experienced vertigo again in a career that is now into its third decade. That frightening episode, however, has added one more page to a book already filled with valuable lessons and memorable aviation experiences.

Dhanee (goodbye), Maldives!

13

"Fish and potatoes... and potatoes and fish"

As a college student in the U.S. during the early 1980s I clearly remember references to the Soviet Union as the "Evil Empire." The cold war was still in full swing and the fear of a nuclear confrontation between the two superpowers and their respective allies was ever present. I vividly remember when an Asian passenger airliner flying from Anchorage to Seoul with 269 passengers and crewmembers was shot down by a Soviet fighter pilot when it inadvertently entered Soviet airspace. Like a lot of people, I was outraged. As a Venezuelan national living and studying in the U.S. it really wasn't my war but I seriously considered joining the U.S. Marine Corps. I felt helpless and desperately wanted to be in a position to kick the Soviet Union's ass. Marines are a tough bunch and the Corps seemed like the best way for me to do my part against Soviet aggression. The only thing that held me back was my fervent desire to become a professional pilot. Unlike the Marines, I would have had to be a U.S. citizen to join the Air Force or Navy in order to become an aviator. Wisely, I elected to continue my undergraduate studies, complete my flight training, and achieve certification as a professional pilot...but I still wanted to kick their asses!

Fast-forward to 1997, the Soviet Union had already collapsed, nuclear war had been averted, and an opportunity for me to see Russia up close for the first time came up. At the time I was working as a pilot for a Singapore-based company. My First Officer and I had just gone to the U.S. via the airlines to meet colleagues at our U.S.-based sister company, and from whom we were to pick up a Learjet 55 to fly it to Singapore. The route of flight from their base of operations in Teterboro, New Jersey, would take us to Seattle, Anchorage, Petropavlovsk (Russia), Osaka (Japan), Taipei (Taiwan) and on to Singapore. Due to the long duty periods two overnight stops were required. The first overnight was planned in Anchorage, Alaska. The second one would ideally have been in Osaka after a required fuel stop in Petropavlovsk. However, the thought of spending the night in Russia, and seeing what it was like, was too tempting to pass so I asked the dispatcher to plan the overnight in Petropavlovsk instead of Osaka. An added advantage of the overnight in Petropavlovsk was that the overall cost was much lower than in Osaka.

The Petropavlovsk airport was primarily an old Soviet Air Force base that had served as a staging point for fighter jets and bomber aircraft carrying nuclear weapons to be ready to attack the U.S. during the cold war. After the collapse of the Soviet Union, Russia's economy was in disarray so the need to attract foreign currency forced Russia to open the Petropavlovsk airport to foreign civil aircraft whose range did not permit non-stop flights from North America to Asia. Our Learjet 55 did not have the range to fly non-stop from Alaska to Japan and Petropavlovsk was suitably located as an ideal fuel stop.

After spending the previous night resting in Anchorage, we conducted the aircraft pre-flight inspection, reviewed the flight plan and weather conditions, refueled the aircraft, and obtained our air traffic control clearance. After an on-time departure, we were promptly identified on radar and cleared to climb unrestricted to our cruise altitude of FL390 (39,000 feet). It was a beautiful early spring day and the gorgeous mountainous landscape below us was astonishing. An hour later we left land behind and found ourselves staring in all directions at the cold and deep North Pacific Ocean. Another hour went by before the Anchorage air traffic controllers handed us over to Russian controllers. It was difficult to understand them due to their strong accent, but they seemed friendly and professional. As we reached landfall the sight of snow-capped mountains and volcanoes was absolutely breathtaking. The airport is located in a bay and the approach is made over the water onto a 10,000-foot long runway. As the wheels touched down and we rolled down the concrete runway, the aircraft shuddered as if it was coming apart. Russian military runways are built from large square sections of concrete joined together that are easily replaceable in case of damage caused by enemy bombing. Russian planes have undercarriages suitably designed to handle these runways using multiple, large and wide, low pressure tires on each landing gear strut. In contrast, the Learjet's narrow and small tires were simply no match. I knew there was no such thing as smooth runways in Russia, but the roughness of the runway took us by surprise. Welcome to Russia!

As we exited the runway we saw a couple of military vehicles. One of them stood before us and led the way to our assigned parking stand. The other one drove some distance behind us and its purpose was to make sure that we did not allow anyone to get out of the aircraft as we taxied in. As we continued taxiing towards the main apron we came across many bunkers with fighter jets and bombers in them. These, now rusty and in decay, were once the front line of attack airplanes that had been ready to take to the sky on short notice in the event of war with the U.S. It was a very strange feeling to see them up close…and to imagine what it would have been like had the cold war turned hot.

At our assigned parking stand we were met by a female ground handling agent who spoke decent English and came across as a tough, thick skinned, and no-nonsense woman. Arrival procedures were uneventful and we were taken to the airport hotel which was intended primarily to accommodate Russian aircrews. The hotel was unlike any hotel I had ever seen. There was no lobby, no valet parking staff, bellboy or even a front desk…just another tough, thick skinned, no-nonsense woman who gave us our room keys and dryly said, "Dinner at seven o'clock." The room was bare but comfortable. There was a bed, a bathroom, a radiator-type heater, and a window facing ugly looking buildings...and that was it. After a much needed hot shower and a change of clothing it was time for dinner so I headed downstairs inside what appeared to be the oldest, and most antiquated, elevator I had ever seen. My First Officer was already there and from the look on his face I could tell that he was seriously questioning my desire, and wisdom, to spend the night in Petropavlovsk instead of modern Osaka. There was no restaurant and there weren't any menus either...just a few tables and uncomfortable chairs. The same grumpy woman sat us down and without saying a word disappeared into the kitchen. She returned a few minutes later with a couple of plates of fish and potatoes. We did not dare to ask for anything else and she certainly did not make an effort to offer anything else either. With dinner over we each returned to our respective rooms and got ready to spend our first, and possibly only night ever, in that part of Russia.

After a good night's sleep, I woke up refreshed and ready for breakfast. I met my First Officer downstairs and, strangely enough, the same woman we had seen the night before. When we asked about breakfast she looked at us with annoyed surprise and asked, "Did you request breakfast with reservation?" To which I said, "I don't know whether our company did or not." She grumpily explained that they don't store food and only go and purchase from the market what they expect to serve each day based on previously received requests. She must have taken pity on us because she said in her heavily accented English, "Have seat. I go to kitchen and see what I can do." A few minutes later she returned with two plates of fish and potatoes that looked very similar to what we had the night before. In fact, I was certain that it was exactly what we had had the night before. At that point I was seriously questioning my own decision, and judgment, about spending the night in Petropavlovsk. I certainly wasn't expecting blueberry pancakes or cheese omelets for breakfast...but I definitely wasn't expecting fish and potatoes leftovers from the night before. Not wanting to offend her we each finished our respective meals and expressed our gratitude. Without so much as a smile, or even a word, she waved us off. With our first meal of the day behind us it was then time to check out. This consisted simply of returning the room keys to her as everything had been pre-paid before arrival. When the ground handling agent arrived at the hotel to pick us up we then proceed to the airport.

A couple of hours later as we were taxiing to the runway in preparation for departure the same two military vehicles escorted us. This time the purpose of the vehicle behind us was to ensure that we did not let anyone board the aircraft as we taxied out. Once the control tower cleared us for takeoff we entered the runway, lined up with the centerline, advanced the thrust levers to takeoff power and, as we accelerated down the rough concrete runway, the aircraft began to rattle. Like the previous day it felt as if the aircraft was coming apart. As the landing gear left the ground the rattling ceased immediately and everything became very smooth. It was a very strange sensation and one that I won't forget. The rest of the trip to Singapore via Osaka and Taipei was uneventful but it was that overnight in Petropavlovsk that has stayed in my memory to this day. After all, we had just had Russian style fish and potatoes for dinner…and potatoes and fish for breakfast, all of it served by a grumpy and no-nonsense Russian woman who took pity on us.

Spacibo (thank you), Russia!

14

A walk on a red carpet

WHILE THE VAST MAJORITY OF my flying in Singapore involved air ambulance flights, for a couple of years we also operated two Challenger 601 intercontinental business jets. These aircraft were specially suited to accommodate up to a dozen business executives in comfort and style. The Learjet's demanding air ambulance trips kept me super sharp while the Challenger's business-style trips gave me the opportunity to go to nice destinations...as well as the time to enjoy them. I loved the variety. One such trip was to Guam, a U.S. territory in the Pacific Ocean.

Early one afternoon one of our dispatchers informed me about a sudden charter request in which we were to fly to Ho Chi Minh City, formerly known as Saigon, in Vietnam, to pick up a movie actor and fly him to Guam. Because of the short notice my focus was on flight planning so I did not really pay much attention to who the passengers were. A couple of hours later we departed Seletar airport aboard N215GA, a Challenger 601-3R, towards Ho Chi Minh City. During the flight our Flight Attendant came to the cockpit and, with the passenger manifest in hand, asked whether one of our passengers was an actor from a popular 1980s TV series about vice detectives. "Could be," I said. With refueling done, arrival /departure procedures completed, and aircraft ready for departure, we stood ready for the arrival of our mystery passenger and his entourage. Shortly thereafter a stretch limo, escorted by various other vehicles, pulled up by the aircraft and a person we quickly recognized as the popular actor got out of his limo and walked up to the aircraft. It turns out a large restaurant chain was opening a restaurant in Guam and, as it was their tradition, a famous Hollywood actor would be there for the ceremony. The five and a half hour trip to Guam across the South China Sea, over the Philippines, and into the Pacific Ocean was uneventful. The welcoming party awaiting our famous passenger seemed like a zoo. There were dozens of vehicles and quite a few people eagerly waiting to take a look at him. Shortly thereafter a Gulfstream IV arrived from Los Angeles via Honolulu with yet another Hollywood actor. Although I had seen him in two Academy award winner movies, I did not really know much about him at the time. Eventually I would become a big fan and enjoy watching many of his movies, especially the hilarious *Two and a Half Men* TV series.

The next day our ground handling agent, a friendly guy who had been living in Guam for several years, came over to our hotel and offered to show us around the island. When I asked him why he had moved to such a remote place he simply said that it was the farthest from the continental U.S. he could get without the need to have a passport. Despite my curiosity I decided not to ask whether he was trying to get as far away as possible from a jealous or spurned lover. A tour of Guam revealed that it was a beautiful island with a very relaxed atmosphere and popular with Japanese tourists. Like most islands and countries in South East Asia, Guam had been occupied by the Japanese Imperial forces during World War II. Eventually, the U.S. Navy retook the island but a few Japanese soldiers remained hidden in the mountains even after the war ended. These soldiers did not know that a pair of atomic bombs dropped over Hiroshima and Nagasaki in 1945 had finally forced Japan to surrender. There were numerous sightings of these ragged looking Japanese soldiers over the years and efforts to bring them down from the mountains were mounted. These usually involved former soldiers, or family members, who used loud speakers to call on them and inform them that the war was indeed over and that it was OK to come down. Despite these efforts there were three Japanese soldiers who stayed hidden in the mountains until 1972, a full twenty eight years after the U.S. regained control over Guam. One of them was Shoichi Yokoi who had been hiding in an underground jungle cave and would eventually be the last remaining Japanese soldier to survive while in hiding (the other two died during a flooding). Yokoi, who had been a tailor before the war, survived by hunting at night and made clothing, bedding, and storage implements using native plants. Apparently he had known since 1952 that the war was indeed over but he feared coming out of hiding because "We Japanese soldiers were told to prefer death to the disgrace of getting captured alive." While out of his cave on a hunting trip he came across a couple of natives and attacked them. The natives managed to subdue him and handed him over to the authorities. It's truly remarkable how this aging soldier, even in peacetime, would not surrender or go down without a fight. Eventually he returned to Japan to a hero's welcome, got married, and took his beautiful bride on their honeymoon to the one place he had spent more than half of his life…Guam! This time however, and fortunately for his new wife, he stayed at a comfortable hotel. After living in caves for so long that must have been quite a change for him though.

 We received an invitation from our passenger's personal assistant to attend the Planet Hollywood opening ceremony that was to take place the night before we were originally scheduled to depart Guam. That is how a Singaporean Flight Attendant (ex-Singapore Airlines and model), a tall and handsome Irish First Officer, and a not so tall and definitely not as handsome Venezuelan Captain found themselves walking down a red carpet while the video cameras rolled and the camera flashes lighted up the night. The hundreds of smiling and screaming people eager to see celebrities walking down the red carpet were probably left to wonder, "In which movie have I seen those two actors and that gorgeous actress?" Not wanting to disappoint them, we enthusiastically waved, smiled, posed…and came close to signing a few autographs! It turns out we were not such bad actors after all.

Needless to say, we had a fantastic time that evening…and to top it off, my smooth talking First Officer was actually offered a small part in a movie by some producer who obviously had had a lot to drink. In the producer's defense, not only did my First Officer look and sound like a real movie star but he was really good at playing the role of an actor just having a great time.

The departure from Guam was extended at our passenger's request so we had a chance to continue enjoying the local sights. Two days later we departed Guam for Macao where our famous passenger boarded a commercial flight bound for China. Shortly after dropping him off we returned to Seletar airport, our home base. On the flight back, my crew and I kept talking and laughing about the trip…and in particular our short-lived careers as actors. Between the remarkable Shoichi Yokoi story, our famous actor, and the party, this had definitely been an enjoyable trip.

Thank you for the fond memories, Guam!

15

Forest fires in Indonesia

FOR SEVERAL MONTHS IN 1997 the skies over most of Southeast Asia were covered with a thick layer of smoke and haze. This man-made disaster was caused by Indonesian farmers when they had set large areas of land on fire. The resulting smoke spread with the wind and wrecked havoc in several countries. Singapore, where we lived at the time, was not spared and we found ourselves breathing foul smelling and poisonous air. So why, and how, did a bunch of Indonesian farmers manage to make the sun disappear and for so long?

Well, I did not know it at the time, but setting fields on fire was a common practice employed by Indonesian farmers as the cheapest and easiest means to clear and prepare their land for agriculture. This technique is called "slash and burn." When you consider the significant number of farmers who began slashing and burning about eight million hectares of land at about the same time, plus the effect of the prevailing wind, the end result was the second or third largest forest fire in recorded history. The economic impact of these forest fires on Malaysia, Singapore, Brunei, Indonesia, and Thailand was estimated to be approximately six billion dollars. Ironically, the country most negatively affected economically by the farmers' "slash and burn" technique was none other than Indonesia itself.

There were times when the pollution index reached dangerous levels and people were encouraged to stay indoors and to avoid extraneous physical activities. During these periods we followed the government's recommendations and stayed home. Interestingly enough it was during one of these occasions that I learned two curious things. First, restaurants and shops offering pizza delivery service and VHS rentals were doing quite well as demand skyrocketed. People were staying at home so it was easier, and safer, to have fast food delivered to your door than it was to go to the markets to buy food. One day we ordered two pizzas, one with mushrooms and green peppers and another with ham and pineapple. After eagerly waiting for nearly 60 minutes due to the high demand our two large pizzas arrived. That's when I learned the second thing. When we opened the boxes we noted that the pizzas looked a little too pink. It turns out that unless you specify that you want tomato sauce they will use Thousand Island salad dressing instead. I may not be a full Italian but I am Italian enough to know that you just don't do that. Mamma Mia! That's almost as bad as punching your mother in the face!

The forest fires severely affected our flight operations due to the resulting low visibility conditions. After all, if you couldn't see the runway, you couldn't land. So before we accepted any trips we carefully reviewed the weather forecast for our destination and alternate airports as well as for our return to our home base airport. If the visibility was forecasted to be too close to the minimum required for the available instrument approach procedure we did not accept the trip. Compounding this situation even further was the fact that Seletar airport, our home base, did not have a published instrument approach procedure, so we had to ensure that the visibility would be such that we could execute a visual approach upon our return. As a precaution we took steps to always carry extra fuel and paid particular attention to visibility trends.

We flew numerous trips during these challenging conditions but there is one trip in particular that I won't forget. We had received a charter request for a trip departing from Singapore's Changi International Airport with two business executives who needed to go to Bangalore, India. We would then spend two nights in Bangalore before returning to Changi with a fuel stop in Medan, Indonesia. After dropping off our passengers in Changi we would return to Seletar.

We departed Seletar airport aboard N107AG, a Learjet 35A, and landed at Changi International Airport fifteen minutes later. After landing we taxied to our designated parking stand, shut the engines down, fueled the tanks to their maximum capacity, prepared the aircraft for the four-hour flight to Bangalore, and conducted our pre-departure safety briefing. Once our passengers arrived and boarded we promptly taxied out and were airborne within minutes. After departure we reached our cleared cruise altitude of FL390 (39,000 feet) within twenty-four minutes and accelerated to the planned long-range cruise speed of Mach 0.73. Strong tailwinds resulted in a ground speed of 480 knots. As we climbed initially through approximately 10,000 feet we left below us the dark and gray haze and found ourselves staring at a clear, sunny, and bright day. It was amazing how beautiful and pleasant it was to see blue skies and the sun again!

While crossing the Bay of Bengal we encountered scattered thunderstorms with tops at 45,000 feet but we easily circumnavigated around them at a comfortable and safe distance. Two hours into the flight we requested a climb and were cleared to climb and maintain FL430 (43,000 feet). Weather reports for Bangalore indicated scattered clouds, calm winds, and good visibility. The subsequent approach and landing to the long runway were uneventful. After landing we taxied to our designated parking stand, shut the engines down, and were pleased to see that we had arrived with more fuel reserve than we had planned. We then spent two nights and three days in the crowded and chaotic city of Bangalore where we stayed at a very lavish hotel. It was without a doubt one of the most beautiful hotels in which I had ever stayed.

For the return flight back to Changi, due to the distance involved and strong headwinds, we planned a fuel stop in

Medan, Indonesia. The three and a half hour flight took us through southern India, across the Bay of Bengal, and into northern Sumatra. Medan, like the rest of the country, was also affected by the forest fires and resulting hazy conditions. Prevailing visibility at the airport was forecasted to be at, or just above, the minimum required for a precision instrument approach procedure. My First Officer and I carefully reviewed the weather reports and the arrival procedures, including a detailed review of the surrounding terrain and the minimum safe altitudes (MSA) for the various sectors. Maintaining a high level of situational awareness under these conditions was even more imperative than usual. So we ensured that we knew exactly where we were at all times in relation to the terrain around us, the ground-based navigation facilities, and the airport. Furthermore, we would not descend below the applicable MSA until we were established on track on a portion of the instrument approach procedure. Every heading and altitude instruction we received from the air traffic controller was crosschecked against the navigation chart so as to ensure that we never descended below the applicable MSA for that sector. Once we were established on the Instrument Landing System (ILS), we descended to the Decision Altitude (DA) and saw the approach lights and the runway environment just above the published minimums. The DA is that point of the approach procedure in which the flight crew has to be able to see the runway environment in order to land. Failing to see the runway environment at that point requires that the flight crew immediately abandon the approach and execute a go-around maneuver. When we reached the DA we executed the visual portion of the approach procedure and landed safely.

After landing we taxied to the assigned ramp and parking stand, shut the engines down, and allowed our passengers to disembark and stretch their legs while we conducted the refueling process. One of the passengers looked around, and noting the extremely low visibility, asked me, "How did you find the airport in this weather?" Without entering into too much detail I explained briefly how we execute an instrument approach using ground-based navigation aids and paper charts. When the fuel truck driver and his assistant started to get the hoses ready to fuel our aircraft I was shocked to discover that the fuel truck was marked as containing Avgas (aviation gasoline) instead of the required Jet fuel (Jet A-1) used on aircraft with gas-turbine engines. Avgas is the type of fuel propeller-driven, piston-engine aircraft use. Using the wrong type of fuel would have been catastrophic as the engines would have eventually flamed out in flight. We had to patiently wait for at least twenty minutes before they returned with the correct fuel truck and could commence the refueling process. Once this process was completed we departed Medan for the one-hour flight to Changi. We had plenty of fuel onboard in case of delays in the Singapore area, or if we had to carry out more than one attempt at landing in Changi, and then had to proceed to our alternate airport. The flight to Changi was fortunately uneventful and we dropped off our two passengers who then boarded a commercial flight back to the U.S. It was now time for my First Officer and I to return to our home base. On this particular occasion, the visibility at Seletar airport was marginal but still adequate for a visual approach. The fact that we were very familiar with the area and the local procedures made a big difference.

Haze was still covering most of the region when, barely a week after our fuel stop in Medan, we learned that a Garuda Airlines' Airbus 300 had crashed into one of the mountains surrounding the Medan airport. It was a classic case of Controlled Flight Into Terrain (CFIT) whereby the flight crew crashed a perfectly functioning aircraft into terrain without being aware of the impending collision. This type of accident occurs when the flight crew loses situational awareness of their position in relation to the terrain, obstacles, ground navigation aids, or the airport. Unfortunately, in those days, aircraft were not equipped with the yet-to-be developed Enhanced Ground Proximity Warning System (EGPWS) which would have given the flight crew advance warning of approaching terrain prompting them to execute an escape maneuver. According to the accident investigation report the flight crew turned right, instead of left, as instructed by the air traffic controller who was himself confused with another aircraft with a similar call sign. The flight crew then received instructions to descend to an altitude that was below the minimum safe altitude for the sector they were in. None of these actions on the part of the flight crew, or the air traffic controller, were intentional, but rather were the result of a series of unfortunate events which created a great deal of confusion.

When I learned about the accident it shook me up. After all, we had been there just a week earlier under identical weather conditions. This was the worst aviation accident in 1997 and the fourth in terms of the number of fatalities involving an Airbus 300. Other than to say that an accident is the result of a series of errors I won't speculate as to what the flight crew should have or shouldn't have done. We call this series of errors the error chain. Each error adds a link to the chain. It usually takes four or five identifiable errors in the chain to cause an accident. The accident is preventable because a chain is only as strong as the weakest link. All we have to do as pilots is to break one link in the chain and the accident won't happen. This accident, like many others before it, would serve as yet another lesson for all pilots that, as human beings and in spite of all the technological advances in our industry, we are still the weakest link in the system.

The haze continued for several more months but enough domestic and international pressure was eventually exerted on the Indonesian government, forcing them to reign in the farmers' slashing and burning. Many countries sent specialized equipment and personnel to assist the Indonesian government in this monumental task. Fortunately the fires were brought under control and eventually the skies started to clear. These forest fires are an excellent example of the cause and effect principle.

As for me, I worked to minimize the risks by carrying extra fuel onboard, carefully reviewing the weather reports, carrying out a detailed briefing with my crewmember, crosschecking the air traffic controller's instructions, and maintaining a high level of situational awareness at all times. Incidentally, there were two times during this dreadful period when I had to initiate and execute a go-around maneuver. On both occasions it happened on arrival into Seletar airport when I either momentarily, or completely, lost sight of the runway while in the traffic pattern coming in for a visual landing. I was certainly glad, and relieved, when those hazy and depressive days were over. There was nothing like the sight of a clear, sunny day!

On a lighter note there is another important lesson from this horrible period that I have tried to always remember. When ordering a pizza in Singapore don't forget to tell them "No Thousand Island dressing, lah!" Not only does a pizza taste a whole lot better with the traditional tomato sauce, but I personally wouldn't want to insult any Italian ancestors, dead or alive, that I may have. Otherwise they would say, "Fuori come un balcone," an expression used to refer to those who are completely out of their minds!

16

The fall of a Giant

THE VAST MAJORITY OF THE flying I did while I was based in Singapore involved air ambulance missions to retrieve expatriates or tourists in need of medical attention and whose medical insurance policy included an evacuation provision. A very large percentage of those missions were flown to and from Indonesia. As a result I had the opportunity to fly to just about every airport, large or small, across this vast country of over two hundred and fifty million people. It never occurred to me that one day I would get a call from our Dispatch office informing me about a series of trips we would be flying to Jakarta, Indonesia's capital, but for a completely different purpose. This time, we would not be flying in with a medical team to retrieve a patient. Instead we would be flying frightened families trying to leave Indonesia…in a hurry.

Large sections of Jakarta and several other major cities across the country were going up in flames and a particular ethnic group was also being targeted: the local Chinese minority. It did not matter that the Chinese minority were, for all intents and purposes, just as Indonesian and patriotic as the rest of the country's citizens. Anger towards them had been brewing for a long time and all it took was a spark – fires were soon burning throughout the cities and in Chinese-owned supermarkets and businesses. Foreigners living in Indonesia, and tourists visiting this beautiful and otherwise friendly country, were completely frightened to see large mobs rioting and burning everything in their path. So what triggered this unfortunate and dramatic event, and why were the Chinese people targeted?

For many years, numerous generations of Chinese people elected to emigrate to various countries around the world as a way to escape poverty. These Chinese immigrants were very hard working and supportive of each other. Regardless of which country they went to these Chinese families often spent their lives working tirelessly on the family business, and eventually many reached a level of financial prosperity that usually surpassed that of the local majority. In Indonesia, as is the case in many other countries, the local Chinese population comprises a very small percentage (3-5%) of the total population. Being a minority, with their own culture and religion, resulted in a certain level of resentment against them. When you add the wealth factor into the equation it isn't very difficult to understand why they were unfairly considered the scapegoats as the national economy melted down. That is exactly what happened in 1998 at the height of the Asian financial crisis.

A number of Asian countries that had been reasonably prosperous in previous years, despite having less than solid economic foundations, were caught unprepared for the 1997-1998 financial crisis. These countries were hit particularly hard. One by one, in what resembled a chain reaction, their currencies lost considerable value and, in one particular case, became nearly worthless. Inflation and food shortages went up, foreign investment dried up, and unemployment skyrocketed. Such was the case with Thailand, Malaysia, the Philippines, and perhaps even more so than any of these countries, Indonesia. None of these ailments were caused by the local Chinese minority in Indonesia. The Asian financial crisis however, brought considerable pain to bear on a population that had already been struggling and suffering for too many years. That, plus a repressed resentment towards the prosperous and culturally different Chinese minority, was all it took for the fires to begin.

After concluding that Jakarta's Halim International Airport was well protected and that it would be safe for us to land, my First Officer and I departed Seletar airport aboard N850GA, a Learjet 36, on the first of many round trips that we would fly in the following days. The one hour and fifteen minute trip was uneventful, but as we started our descent and approached the Indonesian shoreline we noted something over the city we had never seen before. There were tall columns of black smoke rising over numerous parts of the city. It looked like a war zone, and to a certain degree…it was.

After landing we taxied to our designated parking stand where we met a familiar face, the local ground handling agent we had known and used for years. His usual friendly demeanor did not betray any fears or concerns for what was happening to his city and country, but I suspect he realized that although business would boom for him in the following few days it would soon be severely disrupted by the aftermath of the turmoil.

The first group of passengers were ready to board and I could sense and see the fear in their faces. It was an expatriate American family of six who left all their possessions behind as they rushed to the airport in anticipation of our arrival. As a family man myself I could imagine the anguish this husband, and father of four young children, must have gone through as he watched hordes of angry people ransacking and burning everything in their path. I did the best I could to calm them down and reassured them that we would be safely airborne within minutes. To their kids I gently said, "It's okay. You are safe now." There were many other families like this one and I was happy to make them feel safe at a time when they had felt anything but. Over the next several days we flew at least a dozen times from Jakarta with more frightened expatriates and tourists. Only a small percentage of the local Chinese families chose to leave. For them to leave everything that they had worked so hard for, and for so long, was more difficult…besides, this was their country also. Their courage and resilience is commendable. Once the dust settled they were ready to forgive, rebuild, and move on.

The government was able to restore order through military intervention and the application of force but, in doing so, they unintentionally set in motion a series of events that would have been unimaginable just days earlier. Everyone had always assumed that the President, who had ruled Indonesia for over three decades and had been a very popular leader during the 1970s and 1980s, would continue ruling until the day he died. Instead his era was finally coming to an end. Unfortunately it came at a very high price for the entire population and in particular for the Chinese minority. After the riots there was considerable public outcry for the President to step down and be tried in court. We were witnessing the fall of a Giant. This was a significant historical event that eventually resulted in the disbandment of a failed totalitarian and corrupted system and the birth and implementation of a democratic one. This was history in the making... and I was there to see it all happen!

17

"There is problem. Need come Monday."

ONE FRIDAY AFTERNOON I RECEIVED a phone call which forced me to face one of my worst fears: not being able to continue working as a pilot due to a medical condition and wondering how I would provide for my family. The day before I had gone to a local clinic to undergo a medical examination in order to renew my aviation medical certificate. Everything had gone well, or so I thought, until that dreadful phone call.

This type of medical examination was conducted by a doctor authorized by the Federal Aviation Administration (FAA) to carry out such examinations and to issue, or in some cases deny, a new medical certificate based on the results of the examination. There was a lot at stake on these biannual visits to the doctor and it was not uncommon for us to experience what was commonly referred to as the "white coat" syndrome.

As soon as I walked into the clinic that day and the nurse started placing electrode sensors on my body for the required electrocardiogram (ECG) examination, my heart began to pump faster than usual. Over the years I have tried several methods of relaxation during these tests, including visualizing beautiful and peaceful scenery and taking deep breaths, but they never seem to work for me. The moment I lay down my heart rate begins to accelerate. After the nurse finished measuring my height and weight, completed the eyesight and hearing tests, and took a urine sample…it was time for me to face the man in the white coat with the stethoscope hanging around his neck. This particular doctor seemed courteous and friendly but I was well aware that he held my career in his hands. The doctor reviewed my previous medical records and the results of the eyesight, hearing, and ECG tests and then proceeded to ask me some general questions about my health and fitness habits. He measured and recorded my blood pressure and pulse and then used his stethoscope to listen to my heart while I took deep breaths and exhaled. Once he concluded that I had met the medical standards set forth by the FAA, he handed me a new 1st class medical certificate and said, "See you again in six months." I thanked him, placed the new medical certificate in my wallet, paid the bill, and went home feeling happy and relieved that everything had gone well. As I walked away from the clinic I could feel my heart rate slow down and return to normal.

The following day, a late Friday afternoon, a nurse called me and in her limited and heavily accented English said, "There is problem, need come Monday." Trying to remain calm I asked her, "What is the problem?" She simply answered, "There is problem, need come Monday." Anxious to know what was wrong with my medical examination, and not wanting to wait until Monday to find out, I pressed her for an answer. She struggled to explain but all she could articulate was, "There is problem, need come Monday." Despite my attempts to find out exactly what the problem was, it was obvious that with her very limited command of the English language all she could say was, "There is problem, need come Monday." So it was with deep concern that I resigned myself to say, "Okay, thank you. I will be there on Monday."

After I hung up I kept staring at the phone and my mind began to wonder. What could possibly be the problem? Had there been a problem with the ECG results? Did that mean there was a problem with my heart? Whatever it was, the doctor wanted me to return again so that I could submit myself to another examination. He would then either corroborate that indeed "there is problem" and withdraw the medical certificate or, hopefully, determine that everything was OK and tell me to go home. And thus it began, three days and three nights of utter and complete agony. After I turned away from the phone I looked at my unsuspecting wife and our two young kids. I knew then that I had to control my body language and tone of voice so as to not convey the turmoil I was feeling inside. Did the nurse's phone call informing me that "there is problem" and asking that I return to the clinic on Monday mean that I was about to lose my medical certificate? As much as I tried to dismiss the idea I just couldn't put it out of my mind.

I knew that if I lost my medical certificate I would no longer be able to exercise the privileges of my pilot's certificate (the FAA uses the term "certificate" instead of license). Without the ability to use my pilot's certificate I wouldn't be able to fly. If I couldn't fly I wouldn't be able to do my job. If I couldn't do my job I would be contravening the terms of my employment contract. Without an employment contract I wouldn't be able to work and if I couldn't work I wouldn't be able to provide for my family. I felt as if the sky was falling. So over the following three days and nights I kept having the same reoccurring nightmare…and there was nothing I could do about it except to anxiously wait for Monday to come. Needless to say, it was a very long weekend.

Most pilots are deeply passionate about what they do to the point of not ever wanting to consider doing anything other than flying. Our jobs are very specialized and technical in nature and, as a result, we develop and hone skills that are especially suited to flying aircraft safely from point A to point B. That's a strength as much as a weakness. Our skills, knowledge, and experience are not automatically transferable to non-aviation professions. We know that it wouldn't take much for our flying careers to come to a complete stop but, unfortunately, we tend not to think about it…until an unforeseen event threatens to swiftly end our careers. That phone call one late Friday afternoon, and the subsequent three days and nights of agony, did it for me. The possibility of my career as a pilot coming to an end suddenly became real and I needed to come up with a viable plan B. I made the decision right there and then that I would pursue a Master's degree and acquire a specialization that would allow me to use my existing experience as a pilot to continue working within the field of aviation. If I were not able to work as a pilot then I could possibly work as a Safety or Flight Operations Manager or perhaps even as a simulator and ground school instructor. I started to feel a little bit better just knowing that there would be a contingency plan, a plan B.

That was my state of mind when I arrived at the clinic the following Monday. A different nurse with a slightly better command of the English language was sitting behind the counter and greeted me. As soon as I mentioned my name she quickly said, "Oh yes, you need to submit another urine sample." The first thing that went through my head was, "OK, it's not my heart." Feeling somewhat relieved I asked her, "What was the problem with the previous urine sample?" To which she replied, "Oh, there was a problem so you have to do it again." That did not answer my question so I asked her again, "What exactly was the problem with the previous urine sample?" She then looked at some papers and mumbled something to the effect that there was "some infection," whatever that meant. As I turned around and headed for the restroom with an empty container in my hand I kept asking myself, "Infection? What sort of infection?"

After I was done I sat in one of the uncomfortable chairs in the lounge while anxiously waiting for the results of the newly submitted urine sample. As I waited, the minutes seemed like hours. My mind was still in turmoil when I finally saw the nurse walking towards me. She then casually said, "It's OK. No problem, lah." At that point I was so relieved that all I wanted to do was to get up and walk away from that clinic and return home. That is exactly what I did. It felt like a weight had suddenly been lifted from my shoulders and I was literally walking on air. Although relieved, I knew that it had been a close call. When I returned home I explained to my wife everything that had transpired over the previous three days. She was relieved and happy but scolded me for not telling her about it right away. She was right of course. I then proceeded to tell her about my plan B.

Before and during a flight, pilots plan for a "what if" situation. For example, what to do if an engine fails right after takeoff or during the cruise phase of flight, what to do if the weather at the destination airport goes below the minimums required for the instrument approach procedure, what to do in the event that pressurization is lost while at altitude, what to do if there is a medical emergency in-flight, etc. Pilots train continuously for these and other "what if" situations. Unfortunately most of us don't think about a "what if I lose my medical certificate and can't fly anymore?" scenario. The thought of not being able to fly anymore is simply too painful for us to fathom. Even so, we owe it to ourselves, and to our families, to consider the possibility and to come up with a contingency plan for a "what if" we receive a dreadful phone call on a late Friday afternoon.

Thanks to Embry-Riddle Aeronautical University I now have an excellent plan B in place for precisely such a "what if" scenario. Turn the page and read on!

18

"Ivan, you've been admitted to Embry-Riddle!"

BACK IN THE EARLY 1980s while my brother and I were living and studying in Denver, Colorado, we had the brilliant idea of driving to Daytona Beach, Florida, for spring break. We had heard that the place turned in to a wild beach party so, without much planning, we hopped in his brand new and super cool Mustang sports car and headed out on a crazy adventure. The story of how we got there, how many speeding tickets we got, and what we did when we finally got there 36 hours later is certainly worth telling but I'll save that for a different book and with a more appropriate title.

In addition to the parties at the pools and beach, there was a place I had heard about and wanted to visit. As a student enrolled in Metropolitan State College's (MSC) Aerospace Science program in Denver I had heard of, and was intrigued by, Embry-Riddle Aeronautical University. This prestigious university was widely known among aviators as "The Harvard University of Aviation" and many of its graduates were leaders in the industry, military pilots and high-ranking officers, and airline pilots. It even counted several NASA space shuttle astronauts and engineers as alumni. I was very impressed with its expansive campus and atmosphere. Everywhere I looked smelt of aviation and during my short visit I felt immersed in it. I loved it. We returned to Denver a few days later exhausted and absolutely convinced that flying versus driving was a far better option if we ever decided to go back to Daytona Beach for spring break. In 1985 I graduated with a Bachelor of Science degree in Aerospace Science with a Professional Pilot major and a Business Administration minor. My post-graduation flying career was about to start in earnest...and I could barely wait.

Fast-forward to early 1999, I was living and working in Singapore as a pilot for BizJet Services. As a result of an incident with an aviation medical examination I had made the decision to continue my university studies and pursue a Master of Science degree. There was only one university I aspired to be admitted to: Embry-Riddle Aeronautical University. The challenge was that I was working on the other side of the planet, and was a husband and a father to two young kids. How could I possibly pursue a Master's degree over the course of two or three years and still provide for my family...without putting my career on hold? It turns out that

Embry-Riddle recognized this challenge and had come up with an ingenious solution.

At the time, Embry-Riddle, like many other well-known universities around the world, started offering the opportunity of completing and obtaining a bachelor's or a master's degree via a distance learning program. It was intended primarily for working people living around the planet who couldn't just quit their jobs to go back to campus for a few years to obtain a degree. The classes for the various courses were videotaped so that, regardless of where you lived, you could watch and listen to the professor teaching the class and could even hear the interaction with the students. It was almost as if you were in the same classroom but with the added advantage that you could hit the pause button or rewind the tape as many times as you wanted. In addition, there was regular interaction with the professor and other students via a special website where course assignments were given, posted, and critiqued. All the required books, study guides, and VHS videotapes were shipped to the student and full access to Embry-Riddle's vast digital library was provided for research purposes. All examinations were mailed to an Embry-Riddle-approved proctor who had to be a professor in good standing at one of the local universities where you lived. His job was to administer the examination and then mail it back to the respective course professor at Embry-Riddle so that it could be graded. I was excited about the prospect but first I had to be admitted.

I submitted an application along with various letters of recommendation, detailed professional background information, and authorization for them to request and obtain my transcript from MSC. Admission was very selective and they made it quite clear that a minimum Grade Point Average (GPA) of 3.0 throughout the entire program was required. Failure to maintain such a GPA would result in dismissal from the program and the University. Over the course of several weeks I found myself wondering whether I would be admitted and nervously waited for a response. The letter arrived while I was away on a trip. I called my wife that evening and she announced, "You have a letter from Embry-Riddle, should I open it?" I said, "Yes" and held my breath. "Ivan, you've been admitted to Embry-Riddle!" she announced proudly. It was a very emotional moment and I admit to feeling overjoyed. I felt incredibly honored and proud to join the ranks of Embry-Riddle students. Now that I was admitted to the Master's degree in Aeronautical Science I suddenly felt considerable weight on my shoulders. After all, I had to not only excel in my studies in what would be a very demanding program but I also had to ensure that the performance in my role as a husband, father, and professional pilot, did not falter as a result. And so it began. I had never studied so much, so hard, and for so long…and I loved it.

As a graduate student you are expected to conduct vast amounts of academic research as well as to write numerous scholar-quality research papers. This includes submitting a comprehensive Graduate Research Project (GRP) for review and approval by a GRP committee. In addition to conducting research and writing papers I also devoted a minimum of two hours a day to studying. This went on regardless of whether I had already put in 10-12 hours of work at the office or was flying a trip. My books and research material accompanied me everywhere. When I drove my wife to the supermarket I would sit in a corner to study while she did the grocery shopping. I just couldn't afford to waste any time. Most of my weekends were spent at the University of Macao's library (I had by this time moved to Macao) where I could study uninterrupted for six to eight hours each day. My brain became a sponge but, despite the vast amount of time I spent studying, there were times when I felt it just wasn't enough. In fact, I recall sometimes waking up in the middle of the night worried that I wasn't keeping up with my studies. Examinations consisted of 5 or 6 essay-type questions in which you were expected to fill out at least one page with each answer. There was so much information in my brain that I actually needed plenty of extra paper.

My efforts paid off and I started getting straight As. One day my wife said, "Wouldn't it be nice if you were to graduate with all As?" I was instantly intrigued by her suggestion. It just had never occurred to me to consider such a goal. Could I possibly keep up with the workload and complete every examination, research paper, and course assignment with an A? The thought of graduating from Embry-Riddle with such high marks appealed to me so I decided to do it. In retrospect I should have seriously considered how much pressure I was putting myself under and whether such a monumental effort was really worth it. It's one thing to study hard and get As; it's something else entirely different to study hard knowing that you had to get straight As. And so, two and half years later, having successfully completed all program requirements, I graduated with distinction and was conferred a Master's degree with dual specializations: Aviation/Aerospace Operations and Aviation/Aerospace System Safety. The lowest grade I ever received from any examination was an A minus (A-). In recognition of this achievement I received the following letter from the University's Chancellor in December 2001:

Dear Ivan,

Congratulations on the completion of your master's degree. It is a great feeling of accomplishment to finish something upon which you've worked so hard.

In reviewing the grades of those who are graduating, I find that you have achieved a high level of success in completing the requirements of your degree. I would like to take this opportunity to congratulate you on your attainment of a 4.00 cumulative grade point average (CGPA) in the Master of Aeronautical Science degree program.

Since a 4.00 is the highest possible CGPA you can achieve at Embry-Riddle Aeronautical University, this is an outstanding accomplishment which reflects the hard work and discipline you exhibited throughout your course of study.

Best wishes as you graduate and may the insight and knowledge you have obtained at Embry-Riddle continue to bring you success in your career, both now and in the future.

Sincerely,
Robert J. Conrad, Ph.D
Chancellor, Extended Campus

Graduating from Embry-Riddle Aeronautical University remains my biggest and most challenging accomplishment.

Needless to say, it is the one aspect of my career as a professional pilot for which I am most proud of. The level of effort, commitment, and dedication required was considerable but the sense of achievement I feel today made it all worthwhile. After all, Embry-Riddle is about the pursuit of academic excellence in the fascinating world of aviation/aerospace, and I had wanted to be a part of it since that visit to Daytona Beach so many years before.

In early 2002, I went back to school and enrolled in Embry-Riddle's Corporate Aviation Management Program (CAMP). The CAMP was a 5-module, 23-course program, recognized and promoted by the National Business Aviation Association (NBAA). It was developed at the request of Fortune 500 companies in order to provide current and future aviation managers the tools, skills, and knowledge necessary to effectively manage large Flight Departments with multi-million dollar assets. It took me over two years of non-stop effort to complete this excellent program. I have been able to apply many of the concepts that I learned in the CAMP program and as a result have become a far more effective manager.

In 2011, I received an invitation from Embry-Riddle to apply for admission to its recently introduced Ph.D in Aviation degree. This was the first Ph.D in Aviation ever offered by any university anywhere in the world and it was only fitting that it had been Embry-Riddle, "The Harvard University of Aviation," which led the way. I was intrigued and excited at the prospect of pursuing this new and advanced degree but, at the same time, I had reservations. I was

50 years old at the time so the question on my mind was whether I should devote the following four to five years of my life pursuing a Ph.D for which there would be no significant benefit in my line of work. The emotional side of my brain kept saying, "Getting a Ph.D would be super cool. Imagine that, Dr. Luciani. What a way to cap a remarkable aviation career. What are you waiting for? Go for it!" The rational side of my brain decided to spend a little time conducting a cost-benefit analysis and eventually advised against it concluding that "at your age the high cost and considerable effort required would exceed any potential financial and operational benefits." I wasn't quite sure whether to be insulted by the reference to my advanced age but I had to admit that it was the hard truth. If only I had been five years younger. So, with a heavy heart, I elected to give it a pass and instead decided to save that money for my future, self-financed retirement plan as well as spend the extra time pursuing other less strenuous, but highly satisfying, academic and non-academic activities.

Thank you, Embry-Riddle!

19

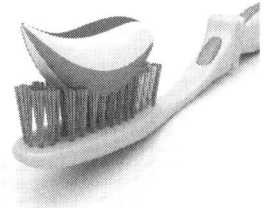

"Did you check the fuel for water contamination?"

ONE AFTERNOON I RECEIVED A call from our Dispatch office informing me that we had an air ambulance trip scheduled for the following day. What was unusual about this particular trip was that instead of going to some remote airport in the region to retrieve a patient and fly him back to Singapore, we would instead be taking a patient from Singapore to Medan, Indonesia. This particular patient had already been given all the medical care he could receive but his condition was considered terminal and his family wanted to take him home. The plan was for us to fly to Medan and, after a one-hour stopover, return to Singapore. The whole trip was scheduled to take six hours so I did not bother taking a small suitcase with a change of clothing or even a toothbrush.

The following day we took off from Seletar airport in N850GA, a Learjet 36. On board was a doctor, a nurse, the patient, and a couple of relatives. The trip to Medan, on the western part of Indonesia, was uneventful. After landing the medical team accompanied the patient and his relatives to a local hospital while my First Officer refueled the aircraft and got it ready for departure. I accompanied the local ground handling agent to the main terminal in order to prepare and submit the flight plan for the return trip as well as to complete several other arrival/departure formalities.

By the time the medical team returned and was on board the aircraft the pre-flight inspection was complete and my First Officer and I had already conducted a pre-departure safety briefing. So, upon receipt of air traffic control clearance and subsequent engine start clearance, we got ready for what we anticipated to be an uneventful trip back home. It was anything but.

For the return flight my First Officer performed Pilot Flying (PF) duties while I undertook Pilot Monitoring (PM) duties. After taxiing to the active runway I lined up the aircraft with the centerline, brought the aircraft to a complete stop, and announced "You have control." My First Officer responded, "I have control." Upon receipt of take off clearance from the control tower he advanced the thrust levers to takeoff off power and we accelerated rapidly down the runway. Once airborne he accelerated to 250 knots as we climbed to our cruise altitude of FL410 (41,000 feet). Passing through 10,000 feet I started to jot down some information on the Operational Flight Plan (e.g., off-the-blocks and takeoff times, fuel on departure, time and fuel over waypoints, estimated time of arrival, etc.). I was busy writing things down when I heard what appeared to be a subtle and brief change in engine sound. I quickly looked up at the engine instruments and saw the right engine's RPM rapidly going back up and matching the left engine's RPM. I did not see my First Officer touch the thrust levers but I asked him, "Did you move the thrust levers?" He said, "No, I didn't." Then I asked, "Did you see the engine's RPM change?" Again he said, "No, I didn't." At that point I decided to put the clipboard away and kept an eye on the engine instruments' indications. As we were passing through approximately 15,000 feet I noticed the left engine's RPM quickly decrease and, just as quickly, go back up to its original setting perfectly matching the opposite engine's RPM. It was then that I knew we had a problem and I thought I knew exactly the cause. So I announced, "I have control." As I commenced a descending, 180 degree left turn I said to my First Officer, "Advise the controller that we are returning to Medan for an immediate landing." We promptly received clearance to proceed direct to the airport and descent to 3,000 feet. During the descent we jettisoned fuel and prepared for a straight in, visual approach. Within 10-12 minutes we were safely on the ground and, as we vacated the runway, I turned to my First Officer and asked him, "Did you check the fuel for water contamination?" He looked at me and nervously said, "No, I did not."

The odds that both engines would display similar discrepancies, and within minutes of each other, is very remote. Nonetheless, other than severe hail damage or flying through a flock of large birds, there are two possible scenarios that could affect both engines at the same time: fuel starvation or fuel contamination. We had plenty of fuel so I knew right away that it was contaminated. That's why the engines started to roll back, however briefly. These engines are very reliable and are designed to run even with a fair amount of contaminants. However, as you climb to altitude, water particles floating in the fuel begin to freeze and, as they do so, the filters get clogged. In case of clogging the filters are automatically bypassed so as to not starve the engines. Unfortunately all of those ice crystals then go through the combustion section of the engine and could potentially cause an engine flameout.

Once at the parking stand we requested that the fuel truck, from which we had refueled, return. When they showed up I asked them to drain fuel samples from the fuel truck and the aircraft fuel tanks and to test the samples for water contamination. The test involves draining a fuel sample from the fuel source into a large glass bottle. Then, using a syringe with a special capsule attached at the tip, draw fuel into it. As the fuel passes through the capsule's yellow filter it turns blue if there are any water particles present. One of our Standard Operating Procedures (SOP) was to always request a fuel sample test from the fuel truck before fueling the aircraft. We even carried our own fuel test kits onboard the aircraft just in case the fuel truck did not have its own kit or its capsules were expired. Upon completion of the test, and confirmation that the capsule's yellow filter had not changed colors, we would intentionally put a drop of saliva on it to ensure that it would indeed change colors. Once we were satisfied that the fuel truck's fuel was not contaminated we would then proceed with the refueling. Unfortunately, on that particular day, the First Officer skipped this important step in contravention of our SOPs and we found ourselves stranded for three days. It could have been a lot worse.

Some years ago a Challenger 601 crashed after both engines flamed out. After their night-time departure the crew was notified that the fuel they had just uplifted had been subsequently found to be contaminated with water. Instead of immediately returning to the airport or landing at the nearest suitable airport, the crew elected to continue to their destination. Fortunately they crash-landed on a cornfield and survived. Incidentally, there is a lot of water between Medan and Singapore. Had we continued climbing, or not realized that we had a problem until much later, we could have ended up ditching in the Malacca Strait. Interestingly enough the cockpit section of that aircraft was salvaged and used to build a Challenger 601 flight simulator. That simulator is located at FlightSafety International's Tucson Center. Years later, after I joined Jet ExecuAir, I attended Challenger 601 recurrent simulator training at that facility and trained in that very same salvaged cockpit. The training center even had an audio recording from the cockpit voice recorder (CVR), commonly referred to as the "black box," in which we could hear the flight crew's frantic voices during the last few minutes before the crash. It was eerie. I heard that CVR recording several times over the years and doing so always took me back to that day in which we departed Medan with contaminated fuel in the tanks.

After arriving in Medan via the airlines our engineers had to drain and clean all the tanks and fuel lines, replace all the filters, and carry out several engine runs plus completing an enormous amount of paperwork. The medical team had to catch a commercial flight back to Singapore and my First Officer and I checked into a hotel for two nights. This was a valuable and unforgettable lesson for my First Officer. These SOPs had been established with a goal in mind: enhancing safety. From that point forward he strictly adhered to them and became a more experienced pilot as a result. Several years later he joined an airline and eventually became a Captain. In that capacity he is now in an excellent position to impart his experience to young First Officers. As for me, I learned another lesson that day: never, ever, ever leave my toothbrush behind, even if I am returning home in just six hours.

20

A mountain between the aircraft and the airport

OPERATING LEARJET BUSINESS JETS IN Southeast Asia for several years in the mid 1990s was very challenging and very demanding, but also very satisfying. We were among the first business jet operators in the region and had to break a lot of ground introducing business aviation to a region where most people had never seen a business jet. I gained a great deal of experience, and believe I contributed in some small way to the implementation of safe operating practices in a region where serious deficiencies existed at the time. Except for a few trips most trips I flew were uneventful. What follows is a brief description of one of those few that was NOT uneventful. It's one that I will never forget for it could have ended in catastrophe had I made a different decision.

We were scheduled to fly several passengers to an Indonesian Air Force base on the eastern part of the island of Java in N850GA, a Learjet 36. We first would have to land in Jakarta's Halim airport in order to clear customs and immigration as well as to refuel. The trip from Seletar to Halim was uneventful and, once arrival procedures were completed, we were airborne again within 45 minutes. The route of flight from Jakarta to the Air Force base was across the scenic island of Java and over a number of active volcanoes. After takeoff we contacted Jakarta Departure Control and were promptly identified on radar and cleared to climb to a cruise altitude of FL330 (33,000 feet). Shortly after leveling off at our cleared cruise altitude, and in communication with an air traffic controller from Jakarta Control, we requested deviation from our cleared route of flight in order to avoid convective activity and its associated turbulence. Our request to deviate around weather was granted and we found ourselves some 20 miles north of the airway as we circumnavigated some rather mean looking thunderstorms. At the Top of Descent (TOD) point, and still off the airway due to the weather deviation, we requested descent clearance. We were subsequently cleared to descend to FL210 (21,000 feet) and instructed to contact the Air Force base controller for further instructions. Once in radio contact with this new controller we were asked to report ready for further descent. I made a mental note that there was no mention of us being identified and in radar contact. As we leveled off at FL210 I could see a layer of solid clouds below us covering all quadrants. When we requested further descend the controller instructed, "Descend 3,000 feet, direct to the airport, expect a visual approach to runway 05." I watched as my First Officer promptly dialed down the Altitude Selector to 3,000 feet while he keyed the microphone to acknowledge the controller's instructions. As we continued our descend and approached the solid layer of clouds a red flag in my head told me to stop the descent and reassess our position in relation to the airport and the terrain below. Because we were off the airway we no longer had a published minimum safe descent altitude. Instead, all we had was a figure that indicated the highest terrain altitude somewhere within a large quadrant of airspace, as depicted on the enroute chart. I stopped descending just above the undercast layer of clouds as I considered that we were not in radar contact, we were off the airway, there was mountainous terrain below and around us, and we couldn't see the obstacles. Having previously reviewed the enroute weather chart I knew that there were scattered clouds forecast to the north of the airport and that would allow us to maintain visual separation from clouds and the terrain. So I made the decision to level off and maintain altitude, slow down to 200 knots, and proceed to an area approximately 50 miles north of the airport. We informed the controller of our plans and he asked us to advise when ready for further descent. As we approached that area to the north of the airport the weather cleared and we could now see the terrain below, so we continued to descend as we turned towards the airport. While we executed a visual approach to runway 05 I looked towards the area where we had initially been coming from when I decided to stop the descent. What I saw shook me up. Between the airport and our off-the-airway position, as the controller instructed us to descend to 3,000 feet, there was a 7,000-foot mountain with its summit partially obscured by clouds.

After landing we taxied to our parking stand, opened the main cabin door, and the passengers got off the plane. When I deplaned I noticed that my legs were shaking. I then spent the next few minutes explaining to my First Officer what had happened. It was now clear to him that had we blindly accepted the controller's instructions to descend to 3,000 feet in Instrument Meteorological Conditions (IMC) while being off the airway and not in radar contact we would have slammed into that 7,000-foot mountain in what is called a Controlled Flight Into Terrain (CFIT) accident. I suspect that when the controller cleared us to descend to 3,000 feet, proceed direct to the airport, and to expect a visual approach to runway 05 he must have assumed that we were in Visual Meteorological Conditions (VMC). Such an assumption had been incorrect and the consequences of that error could have been catastrophic.

There is a term used in aviation called Situational Awareness (SA), which is defined as having an accurate mental picture of what is happening around you, and in particular, where you are at all times in relation to obstacles and terrain. That day we had a partial loss of SA and, in the process, added one more link to the error chain that, if not broken, could have led to a CFIT accident. We broke a link in the chain and prevented the accident when the controller's well-intended instructions to proceed direct to the airport and to descend to 3,000 feet were not immediately followed. The reason why my legs were shaking after landing was because I knew what would have happened if we had failed to realize that something was amiss. We were very fortunate and gained a great deal of experience that day, experience which I have strived to share with many others so that they won't find themselves in a situation in which there is a mountain between the aircraft and the airport.

21

Special deliveries in Southeast Asia

THERE IS A SMALL KINGDOM located in Asia with a population of half a million people. The country is modern and stable, and its citizens enjoy a high quality of life. This includes receiving free medical care and education, and being exempted from having to pay income tax. The country's vast oil and natural gas revenues have made it one of the richest countries in the world. Its ruler is one of the richest men in the world.

During the approach to landing at the country's International Airport the King's beautiful Palace can be seen out in the distance. As expected, it is an enormous structure which, according to a google search, has hundreds of rooms, a garage large enough for over one hundred vehicles, and even an air conditioned stable for the King's polo ponies. As if that isn't impressive enough it is also reported to be one of the largest residential palaces in the world. After landing you can see the King's two huge hangars, where his personal jets are housed. Several years ago he had an impressive fleet comprised of several airliners, ultra-long range executive business jets, and helicopters. Interestingly enough the King is not just an aviation enthusiast and owner. He is also an avid aviator who frequently flies his personal aircraft on state visits. I find that absolutely remarkable. After all, there aren't that many world leaders who could make a similar claim. Although he is accompanied at the controls by experienced professional pilots the King is obviously a very capable pilot himself.

I have flown quite a few trips to this country over the years, including one with a member of a European Royal family – red carpet and honor guard reception and all. During one overnight I had the opportunity to stay at a hotel built by the King for an international meeting a year earlier. This was among the most beautiful and expansive hotels I have had the pleasure of staying in. Every guest room was larger than your traditional hotel suite and even the bathrooms were larger than a typical one-bedroom apartment in Hong Kong. I can only imagine what the suites must have looked like. It was surreal to say the least and I found myself not wanting to check out. Although most of the trips I have flown to this country were typical passenger charter flights, there were a couple of unusual trips that are definitely worth mentioning. These trips began with a peculiar phone call from our Dispatch office. One such call went like this: "Captain, there is a trip tomorrow afternoon at 2 PM departing from Changi. Pick up three passengers arriving from London via an airline, fly them to XYZ, wait for them for one hour, and then fly them back to Changi. They will then spend the night in Singapore and catch the next commercial flight back to London." OK, I thought. All the way from London just to spend an hour on the ground and then go back? I couldn't help but wonder what that was all about. The answer to that question would soon be revealed.

The following day my First Officer and I departed Seletar airport at 12:30 PM in N850GA, a Learjet 36, and landed fifteen minutes later at Changi International Airport, Singapore's main airport. After landing we taxied to our designated parking stand at the apron and shut the engines down. With typical Singaporean efficiency the ground handling agent provided me a folder containing all required documents and advised that the passengers had just arrived from London and were being escorted through customs and immigration. Arrival at the aircraft was estimated at 1:45 PM. A quick review of the documents revealed the flight plan, weather package, Notices to Airmen (NOTAMs), and crew and passenger General Declaration forms. My First Officer had already started refueling the aircraft and was getting it ready for departure. Shortly before the passengers were due to arrive the ground handling agent returned and handed me a stamped custom form. He then asked me to please review it. It indicated that a load of precious gems, valued at several million dollars, had been declared by one of my passengers.

The bus carrying our three passengers pulled over by the

aircraft; they disembarked and, after a brief greeting, got on board and took their seats. Their appearance and demeanor clearly indicated they were not executives on a typical business trip. These gentlemen were deliverymen on what was obviously a sensitive mission – and they looked tense. The lead passenger was holding a metal attaché case. Nothing unusual about it except it was handcuffed to his wrist, not something we see very often. His two companions, muscular guys sporting crew cuts, were clearly ex-military. Their swagger and appearance suggested Special Forces. These were the bodyguards. It was apparent that, under the protection of his two bodyguards, the lead passenger's job was to hand deliver those precious gems. Our job would be to fly them to their destination, safely and promptly, so they could complete the delivery.

Once the cabin door was closed I introduced myself, welcomed them aboard, provided a pre-departure safety briefing, and told them about the in-flight catering. I then joined my First Officer in the cockpit. Air traffic control clearance for the one hour and thirty minute flight was requested and received. Engine start and taxi clearance to runway 02L were subsequently requested and received. Within minutes we were cleared to enter the runway and authorized for takeoff. We lined up the aircraft with the centerline, advanced the trust levers to takeoff power, and commenced accelerating down the 13,000-foot runway. Once airborne we turned eastbound as we climbed to a cruise altitude of FL410 (41,000 feet). Twenty five minutes later we leveled off, accelerated to Mach 0.80, and began briefing the approach and landing procedures. We would be on the ground in an hour. During the entire flight the passengers did not utter a single word to us, or even among themselves. They didn't help themselves to the in-flight catering or drinks either. I could sense the tension in the air. They looked at us, and everything we did, with polite suspicion. That demeanor was clearly understandable considering what they were carrying, and the region we were in.

The approach and landing were uneventful and, after we taxied to our parking stand and shut the engines down, our passengers disembarked and were promptly whisked away by, what I presumed, was a security team. An hour later our three passengers were back on board minus the metal attaché case and its precious contents. Having started their journey in London many hours earlier they looked completely exhausted. However, with their delivery mission successfully completed they now looked somewhat relaxed and ready to return home. On the flight back to Changi they allowed themselves a bite to eat before sleeping soundly the rest of the way. I flew two of these unusual delivery trips within a few months and was glad when there were no more of them.

Another special delivery flight similar to the one above involved a pop up charter to deliver a set of golf clubs. No handcuffs or bodyguards required this time, just a relaxed and far more sociable individual whose job it was to hand-deliver the golf clubs in the middle of the night. A very special set of golf clubs, no doubt, and hopefully, one heck of a good game of golf the following morning!

22

Cannibalism, gold, and glaciers

INDONESIA IS THE LARGEST AND most populated country in Southeast Asia. The archipelago consists of some fifteen thousand islands spread across over three thousand miles and boasts a population of over two hundred and fifty million people. As a Singapore-based Learjet pilot flying air ambulance missions as well as passenger charter trips I had the opportunity to see everything from active volcanoes, majestic mountains, beautiful sandy beaches, dense jungles, large rivers, and even glaciers. There is a place in particular that I'll never forget. It's called Timika.

Timika is located in Irian Jaya, a province in eastern Indonesia that occupies the western half of the island of New Guinea. Formerly known as West New Guinea, it had been a colony of the Netherlands from 1828 until 1962. The territory was then administered by Indonesia until the people voted in favor of reuniting with Indonesia in 1969. In early 1967, a major U.S. mining company based in New Orleans became the first foreign mining company to enter into a contractual arrangement with the Indonesian government for exclusive mining rights in the region. The area is one of the most isolated frontiers on earth and is populated by several tribes. Until just three decades ago these tribes still practiced cannibalism. There was a case in the 1970s of a highland tribe that killed and ate a missionary preacher and a dozen of his assistants. Apparently they had all been deemed guilty of stealing land or taking liberties with the local women. While these tribes still preserve, and practice, most of their ancient traditions, cannibalism does not appear to be as prevalent today as it used to be.

In addition to these tribes the island of New Guinea is also home to one of only five equatorial glaciers in the world. Indonesia's tallest peak, Puncak Jaya (4,884 meters or 16,204 feet), is located here. While its peak is free of ice there are still several glaciers on its slopes. Unfortunately these rare glaciers have been shrinking slowly over the past few decades and will eventually disappear.

Evidence of the existence of copper in the mountains of Western New Guinea was first found during a Dutch expedition in the 1930s. The expedition's objective had simply been to climb Puncak Jaya's peak, not mining. A geologist, who was part of the expedition, came across a large malachite-stained outcrop which he, being Dutch, named Ersberg. That's Dutch for ore mountain. Despite this unexpected discovery, mining in such a remote location was simply not feasible at the time and wouldn't be for many more years. In the geologist's opinion mining in that region would be just as feasible as mining in the moon. In 1960, another expedition headed out to the same area, but with a different objective in mind: finding ore. Eventually they found what they were looking for and concluded that the potential for mining was much greater than they had initially thought. That is how this large mining company embarked on the monumental task of mining in this distant and isolated area. But in order to do so they had to first build the necessary support infrastructure. This consisted of a port, an airport, roads, housing, hospitals, a hotel, churches, schools, restaurants, recreational facilities, and everything else needed to make life comfortable, and safe, in a land where cannibalism was still practiced at the time. In addition they had to bring in trucks, tractors, heavy drill and excavation equipment, and everything else necessary to build, operate, and sustain a mine in a very harsh environment.

My First Officer and I departed Singapore's Changi airport aboard N850GA, a Learjet 36, with three mining executives who had flown in from the U.S. via the airlines the day before. The route of flight would take us east of the Malay Peninsula, over the islands of Borneo, Sulawesi, and Maluku, and then on towards New Guinea. We climbed unrestricted to FL410 (41,000 feet) and accelerated to a cruise speed of Mach 0.80. Because of stronger than expected headwinds the flight time ended up taking five hours and five minutes which was the longest I had ever flown a Learjet. This particular Learjet model had a larger tail fuel tank that provided an extra hour of endurance when compared to the 35A but the extra fuel came at the expense of a considerably smaller baggage compartment. Weather enroute was excellent but as we descended towards Timika we couldn't see the famous Puncak Jaya or any of its glaciers because the mountain range was covered with clouds. After an uneventful non-precision instrument approach and landing we taxied to our parking stand, shut the engines down, opened the cabin door, and were welcomed immediately by the area's high heat and humidity. While our smartly dressed passengers were whisked away, we were driven to what I can only describe as a gorgeous hotel built in the middle of the jungle. The hotel, managed by a large hotel chain, was two stories high and had been cleverly designed to blend in with its natural surroundings. The rooms were very comfortable and had all the amenities you would expect of a luxury hotel. What made all of this so impressive was the fact that we were in the middle of a jungle and that absolutely everything was brought over by ship.

The following morning we were picked up at the hotel by an employee from the mining company for a tour of the mining facilities. The tour began by hopping aboard a large, four-wheel drive truck – the only way to tackle the rugged and steep terrain up the mountain. Our destination that day would be the famous mine – the richest and most remote deposit of copper and gold in the world. The ride up the mountain was slow, bumpy, and at times a bit scary due to the steep terrain. Every time the driver had to stop I felt as if we were about to slide backwards. It was obvious, however, that our driver had done this many times and seemed relaxed as he skillfully maneuvered the large vehicle up the trail. As we continued our ride up and through the dense vegetation our driver, who also played the role of tour guide, pointed at what appeared to be a small number of people trekking behind some trees. We could tell that these were people of one of the tribes because of the way they looked and the fact that they were scantily dressed. This was my first contact with members of the local tribes and the first thing that went through my mind was that they practiced cannibalism. Fortunately they did not seem interested but I was eager to put some distance between us. As we drove by they just ignored us and we made no attempt to get closer to them.

Further up the mountain we passed a town where most workers lived in what appeared to be basic but reasonably comfortable accommodations. This small little town had a well-equipped hospital, a school, a church, a mosque, a park, a police station, and even a shopping center. All of this was built in the middle of the jungle and, as our driver pointed out, with material that had to be brought in by ship and then transported with trucks up the mountain. At that point I began to comprehend and appreciate the magnitude of this project. Nothing, however, prepared me for what I saw when we finally reached the enormous, deep, and open pit at the top of the mountain. The circular pit reached deep into the ground by what appeared to be a continuous and descending spiraling road. Towards the bottom of the pit I could see enormous excavation machinery and dozens of the largest trucks in the world, the super-heavy-duty Caterpillar trucks, which are used to move tons of soil. The wheels on these monster trucks are as tall as a two-story building. The first thing that went through my head when I stood next to one of them was to wonder how on earth did they bring these trucks all the way up here. The answer of course, was by ships coming all the way from North America, and then driven up the mountain by very skillful drivers.

In the background, and some distance away, I could see the famous glaciers. It seemed as if I had suddenly stepped into another part of the planet. There I was, in a country located very near the equator and where high temperatures and humidity are the norm and yet we were staring at glaciers! I had previously seen glaciers while flying over Alaska but this was the first time I had ever seen them from the ground. As we absorbed this amazing sight our driver explained that the glaciers had been shrinking at a high rate per year and would eventually disappear completely. "Enjoy this magnificent sight while you can," he said. We did marvel at the sight before us but lamented to hear about their eventual disappearance.

Later on that afternoon we left the dry and cool air of the mountains and embarked on the return trip down the steep and rugged road back to our hotel...and the high heat, humidity, and mosquitoes. If going uphill was a bit scary, going downhill was absolutely frightening. Fortunately the truck was specially designed for this type of terrain and our driver was again very skilled. Nonetheless I breathed a sigh of relief when we finally arrived at the hotel.

After a three-day stay in this remote and dense jungle, we departed Timika on the four hour and a forty five minute westbound trip back to Singapore...and civilization. We climbed unrestricted to a cruise altitude of FL430 (43,000 feet) and accelerated to a cruise speed of Mach 0.77. A couple of hours later we climbed to FL450 (45,000 feet), the Learjet's service ceiling. As we leveled off it occurred to me that on this particular trip I had flown the Learjet the longest I had ever flown it and at the highest altitude it could fly, and to top that, I had just been to one of the most remote locations on earth. What a magnificent experience it was for us to have seen these ancient tribes (at a safe distance!), the largest gold mine in the world...and, perhaps even more importantly, these soon-to-disappear majestic equatorial glaciers.

Selamat tinggal (thank you), Indonesia!

23

Air Ambulance Operations

THE MOST CHALLENGING AND DEMANDING flying I have done in my aviation career so far was when I worked for BizJet Services in Singapore. Most of the flying consisted of air ambulance (medevac) trips flown in Learjet aircraft to some of the most remote locations in the region. We landed at just about every airport in Indonesia, Malaysia, Vietnam, Laos, Cambodia, Myanmar, India, Nepal, and many others.

The challenges, and to some degree the risks, associated with this type of flight operation were considerable: short notice trips to unfamiliar airports, long duty periods, mountainous terrain, night time operations, short runways, no air traffic control radar, lack of precision instrument approaches, unreliable weather reports, and air traffic controllers whose English proficiency level was limited. Our First Officers were fairly inexperienced and were flying their first jet aircraft. The aircraft, Learjet 31, 35A, 36, and 55 were equipped with the most basic navigation, communication, surveillance, and safety equipment. All of these factors left little to no room for error.

To minimize the risks we identified hazards and came up with documented procedures to help us either eliminate or minimize their impact. Standard Operating Procedures (SOP) were developed, implemented, reviewed, revised, and strictly adhered to. These SOPs clearly defined what it was that we did, how we did it and, just as importantly, how we integrated with other departments within the company. As a result the Flight Operations and Maintenance Departments were able to cohesively operate in a safe and efficient manner. Everyone was on the same page and moved towards the same goal. Our operations were coordinated and purposeful. It was absolutely beautiful to watch.

Medevac trips are only scheduled and carried out to retrieve a patient who is stabilized, able to fly, and released for travel by the attending physician. Once we landed at the destination airport the medical team would proceed to the hospital, assess and retrieve the patient, and return to the airport in an ambulance. During their absence the First Officer and I would complete all the arrival/departure formalities, refuel the aircraft, prepare and file the flight plan, conduct a pre-departure briefing, and get the aircraft ready for departure. When the ambulance returned the patient would be transferred to the aircraft and secured to the onboard stretcher. We would normally be given priority for departure and would be airborne within minutes. We flew as fast as we could for as long as we could. Waiting for us after landing in Singapore would be another ambulance ready to promptly drive the patient to one of the top-notch hospitals in the country.

The whole process began at our Flight Dispatch office where the dispatcher on duty would have already done a great deal of work prior to contacting the flight crew: charter agreement prepared and signed, overflight and landing permits secured, flight plan prepared and filed, weather and Notices to Airmen (NOTAM) package requested and collected, local ground handling agent confirmed and notified, fuel purchase orders submitted and approved, ground power unit (GPU) requested, maintenance personnel notified, etc. Then, the call. "Captain, we have a trip to Kathmandu departing in two hours. What time would you like to be picked up?" I would normally have one hour to get ready, be picked up, and arrive at the airport exactly one hour prior to departure. By the time I arrived at the airport maintenance personnel would have already towed the aircraft out of the hangar, parked it at the departure stand, connected the GPU, and carried out their pre-flight inspection checks. The First Officer would be supervising the refueling operation and conducting a pre-flight inspection. I would head to the office first where the Dispatcher would provide me a detailed briefing and hand me the "Trip Package" containing all the required documents associated with the trip: permits, fuel arrangements, ground handling information, passenger information, etc. I would then use a computer to prepare and print out the

Operational Flight Plan. Once at the aircraft the First Officer and I would carry out a pre-departure safety briefing, request air traffic control clearance and, as soon as the medical team arrived and boarded, request engine start clearance.

Typically, two hours after the phone call was received and one hour after we arrived at the airport we would be airborne, climb at 300 knots/Mach 0.75 to our cruise altitude, accelerate to a cruise speed of Mach 0.80, descend at Mach 0.80/300 knots, maintain 300 knots below 10,000 feet (with prior Air Traffic Control approval) until 20 miles from the destination airport and then finally, and quickly, slow down to flap speed for the approach and landing.

The trips were challenging, exhausting, and very risky but we derived an enormous sense of satisfaction knowing that we were doing something to help another human being. That feeling made it all worthwhile. The medical teams, the ground support staff, and my crew and I helped a lot of people over the years. It is, however, the patient we couldn't save that I will never ever forget. It happened on a trip from Hanoi, Vietnam, to Singapore on Valentine's Day. On board we had a gravely ill female patient and her husband. They were a French couple in their early sixties who had been touring Vietnam. Before departure the doctor had confided in me that she was in very critical condition and would probably not make it. My First Officer and I focused on our jobs with mechanical precision while the medical team did their utmost to care for her. I was fully conscious of the importance of getting the patient to Singapore as quickly as possible while simultaneously being aware that external, or self-induced pressure, could lead me to commit errors and that these errors could lead to an accident. During the flight I glanced back at the cabin a few times and was relieved to see the respirator, placed above the patient, move. She was breathing and I felt hopeful that she would make it. Due to prevailing low visibility conditions in the area at the time of our arrival our first approach resulted in a go-around. As I advanced the thrust levers to full power, pitched the nose up, and climbed rapidly away from the ground I was fully aware that precious few minutes, minutes she simply did not have, would be lost…but I had no choice. Deep inside me I knew I had made the right decision to abandon the approach but that did little to assuage how I felt. Fortunately the second approach and landing were uneventful and we did not have to divert to Changi, our alternate airport. After vacating the runway we promptly taxied to the parking stand where an ambulance was standing by. Once we shut the engines down I got out of my seat, went into the cabin to open the main door, and glanced towards the doctor. Our eyes met very discreetly and, in an almost imperceptible manner, he briefly moved his head sideways. She was dead. The ground crew promptly removed the stretcher and placed the patient in the ambulance. The husband, in a very dignified way but with moist eyes, extended his hand, shook mine, and in a cracking voice said, "Merci beaucoup." He then turned around and got in the ambulance. With a knot in my stomach and a heavy heart I stood there watching as it drove away and disappeared. My First Officer and I then completed our post-flight procedures, cleared immigration, and walked back the short distance to our office as our engineers towed the aircraft into the hangar. As Chief Pilot I had my own office so I went in, closed the door and the window shades, sat in my chair...and wept.

These demanding trips kept me super sharp and always on my toes but they also took a toll on me. After a few years I was exhausted and knew I could only go on for so long before I burned out. I was in desperate need for a change. And so, it was very opportune when my young daughter told me, "Dad, you can accept the job." She was referring to a job I had recently been offered with Jet ExecuAir in Macao flying a Challenger 601. I had nearly turned down the job offer when it became apparent that the family did not want to move from Singapore to Macao. Her approval meant I could accept the job and start flying passengers who could actually walk to the aircraft, as opposed to being carried on a stretcher. And that's how the next chapter of my professional career started...and what an experience it was!

24

"Dad, you can accept the job."

WHILE I WAS LIVING AND working in Singapore I came across a rather curious newspaper article that caught my attention. At the time, I was sitting at a bakery enjoying a nice cappuccino and casually reading the local newspaper while patiently waiting for my wife to finish her shopping. I learned that there was a gentleman who was a very wealthy businessman in his late 70s and who was celebrating the birth of his new child. Little did I realize at the time that a few months later I would meet this great gentleman in person, would eventually devote a total of eleven years of my life working for him and, in the process, have the utmost respect for him.

It all started with an e-mail I received in early May, 1999, from Roger Lewis, Aviation Manager for Jet ExecuAir. In his message titled "Challenger Captain Opening" Roger indicated that he was looking for someone with Challenger experience who was already acclimated to living in Asia. He went on to say that Bob, a friend and ex-BizJet Services colleague in Singapore, "spoke very highly of you." This was a very pleasant and timely surprise as the thought of a change appealed to me. So I went to see my boss shortly thereafter, told him about the unsolicited job offer, and that I wanted him to be aware about my intentions to check it out. He thanked me for the heads up and asked me to keep him posted. I discussed the e-mail with my wife and we agreed that I would explore it without making any commitment. I replied to Roger and we agreed to talk on the phone the next day. We hit it off right away. We spoke for nearly an hour and concluded that we shared the same values, principles, and objectives. He then extended an invitation for me to come to Macao for a visit, all expenses paid, and under no obligation on my part to accept the job offer. He seemed eager for me to take a look at Jet ExecuAir's flight operations and hoped that I would be interested.

A few days later I arrived in Macao, was welcomed at the airport by Roger, and then driven to the office to meet all the staff. We then walked over to the hangar and I saw the aircraft, a beautiful and shiny Challenger 601-3R. That evening the entire staff took me out for dinner and bowling. It was obvious to me that this was a close-knit operation. I felt welcomed and quite pleased with what I had seen. Without either accepting or declining the job offer I returned to Singapore the following day with plans to discuss it with my wife, Maree, and the kids. I wanted the job but I had some convincing to do. After all, they had settled down in Singapore a few years earlier and were quite happy living there.

As expected Maree and the kids did not seem open to the idea of relocating to Macao. What little we knew about Macao wasn't all that flattering. I called Roger and told him that, although I was excited about the possibility of working for him, my wife and kids were not entirely convinced about the move. He then asked, "Why don't you bring them over for a visit?" He reiterated that all expenses would be paid for and I would be under no obligation to accept. A couple of weeks later the entire family and I arrived in Macao where we were lodged in a two-bedroom suite at a beautiful hotel and given the royal treatment over the course of three days. It was obvious that Roger was very interested in recruiting me. The family had a great time but were still unconvinced. We agreed to go back to Singapore to think about it.

Over the next few days we talked about it some more but it was obvious that the kids did not want to leave their school and friends to start all over in a new location. In addition life in Singapore was simply very pleasant. We were living in a spacious apartment located in a gorgeous complex with a large pool, jacuzzi, tennis courts, a gym, and surrounded by beautiful gardens. It was hard to compete with Singapore but I was burning out at my current job and was looking forward to a much needed change. Chelsie, our intellectual young daughter, decided to do a comparison analysis in which she wrote on a chart the advantages and disadvantages of Singapore and Macao. I suspect that Macao did not fare all that well in that scientific comparison but a little prodding from my wife, who knew my state of mind, probably convinced my daughter to give me her own approval to accept the job. That is how she came to me and said, "Dad, you can accept the job."

Her timing was perfect. I was just about to call Roger to tell him that I was regretfully going to decline his job offer. With my daughter's approval at hand I promptly called him to tell him that I was accepting the job and was looking forward to joining his team. He was absolutely delighted to hear the news. Three months later I joined Jet ExecuAir as a Challenger Captain and soon-to-be appointed Chief Pilot. We moved to Macao and, within a few weeks, we settled down into a beautiful and spacious apartment by the waterfront and with a great view. Our move to Macao turned out to be the start of a highly rewarding and exciting new adventure.

Thank you Chelsie, Michael and Maree for allowing me to accept this job!

25

The Twilight Zone

BACK IN THE 1960S THERE used to be a science fiction TV series called *The Twilight Zone* that portrayed paranormal events. When I lived in Denver in the 1980s one of the local TV stations had re-runs of these black and white shows. The episodes never appealed to me so I did not actually watch them. Little did I know, however, that years later I was going to personally experience what it was like to go through "The Twilight Zone."

I had recently joined Jet ExecuAir in Macao when I was assigned to fly a three-day trip to Pyongyang, North Korea's capital. Our Chairman held a gaming license in Macao and had been invited by the North Korean government to open a casino in Pyongyang. North Korea, commonly known as the Hermit Kingdom, was then, and still remains, closed to the outside world. However, with their economy in shatters, they were in desperate need for foreign income so a casino was opened to attract Chinese tourists. Gambling in China is not legal but its population loves gambling, has disposable income, and can easily cross the border into North Korea. Unlike most places around the world you can't just fly a business jet into North Korea. The trip was scheduled at the invitation of the government so that the Chairman could attend the casino's opening ceremony…and that's how I found myself entering "The Twilight Zone."

We departed Macao aboard CS-XYZ, a Challenger 601-3R on September 30, 1999, for the four-hour trip to Pyongyang. At the time Macao was still a Portuguese colony hence the aircraft's CS-registration. The route of flight took us north into and through Chinese airspace, past the northern city of Dalian and east into North Korean airspace. The first thing I noticed after establishing radio contact with the North Korean air traffic controller was…silence. There were no other airplanes communicating with the controller on the radio frequency. Approach and landing were uneventful but it felt weird not to hear or see other aircraft in the air or on the ground. We taxied to the ramp and reached our designated parking stand where a large, colorful, and happy-looking welcoming committee awaited to greet us. After dispensing with the arrival formalities, which included surrendering our passports and cell phones, our passengers were whisked away in what appeared to be a fleet of Russian-built limos.

Once we completed the post-flight inspection and the refueling, we were introduced to our guide and a driver. Our guide was a young woman who spoke excellent English. Her job would be to show us around during our stay but first we were taken to our hotel. On the way over I noted several things. First, the streets were nearly empty of people and there were just a handful of cars. Second, the people we saw on the street wore similarly colored types of clothing – mostly dull, light or dark gray colors. Third, there was what looked like either police or military checkpoints every few blocks. Lastly, we noted that our guide spoke to the driver immediately after saying anything to us and did so with deference. It was obvious he was the boss and she had to tell him in Korean everything she or we had said in English.

Our hotel was a tall building built on an island in the middle of the Taedong river that runs through the city. There were no "Hotel" signs on the building, just a plain, 20-story tall building. Our guide escorted us to our rooms, handed us our keys, and told us that dinner would be served at 7 PM in a large room downstairs. The driver did not follow us and I suspected that was because there were probably cameras and microphones recording everything. The room itself was large but bare. Other than a double bed there was a small TV, a closet, the bathroom, and a window that offered a view of the city. Outside I could see wide, but mostly empty streets, low-rise buildings, and the river. Without much to do, and feeling curious, I decided to turn on the TV. There was a single station that at the time was showing a program where people were asked questions and whoever answered correctly won the contest. They were speaking in Korean so I couldn't understand what they were saying but by their body language it was obvious people were animated and having a good time. We've all seen this type of TV program before. Contestants were being shown a picture of an object and were then asked to guess the name of the object. If the contestant answered correctly there would be applause and lots of smiles. What was unusual about this program were the pictures. They consisted of military hardware that I deduced were South Korean and American. There were pictures of Navy ships, aircraft, tanks, etc. I recognized what was obviously a U.S. aircraft carrier. The contestants had to guess the name and type of ship, the type of aircraft or tank, etc. It was all part of the militarization of the people. Even a TV game show had a military purpose.

Dinner was a formal ceremony. There was folk dancing and singing while we ate and drank. It was obvious that our passengers were being given the royal treatment, but it was also obvious that it was propaganda at its best. It looked like an effort to give us the appearance that everything was well and that everyone lived happily. It was all a utopian image. The next day we were picked up early in the morning for a tour of the city. We were taken to see the largest and most magnificent statues, sculptures, and paintings I had ever seen. They were all huge monuments commemorating the life of the Dear Leader and father of the nation, Kim Il-sung. Our guide spoke with a great deal of affection for the Dear Leader and his son, Kim Jong-il, the current Supreme Leader. It was like a granddaughter talking about her loving grandfather and father. We were also driven to see a food store. At the time the international press was reporting that rampant food shortages and famine were afflicting the North Korean people but the government was vehemently denying these reports. The store was closed but what was unusual about it was that all we could and were allowed to see from our van was a large front window and, through it, shelves on the far wall full of food products. They obviously wanted us to believe that, contrary to what the foreign press was reporting, there were no shortages of food in North Korea. Wherever we went our driver was always within earshot and discretely kept an eye on us…and even on our guide. It appeared as if someone was always watching to make sure that no one stepped out of line.

The opening ceremony took place that evening. The casino was located in the basement of the hotel and was rather modest in its size and appearance. There were just a few tables and none of the lights and sounds normally associated with a casino. After this rather brief ceremony we returned to the same large room for dinner. We were again entertained with more folk dancing and singing by beautifully dressed women. At one point we were asked to join them on the dance floor.

The next morning we were driven back to the airport and our unstamped passports and cell phones were returned. There were no delays departing as we were the only aircraft moving on the airport. The flight back took us over the same route of flight towards the Chinese city of Dalian and then south across Chinese airspace towards Macao. We had just left "The Twilight Zone."

Interestingly enough I flew a trip a couple of weeks later to Seoul, South Korea's capital. This trip highlighted the vast contrast between these two countries. Seoul is a prosperous and bustling city with lots of well-to-do people, streets filled with new cars, tall modern buildings, large shopping centers, and lights everywhere. Another interesting fact is that its people are considerably taller than its neighbors to the north. This is probably because of better nutrition and medical treatment. As I looked out the window of my luxurious hotel room towards the north I remembered that "The Twilight Zone" was a mere 20 miles away and I had gone through it. There weren't that many foreigners back then who could say that.

26

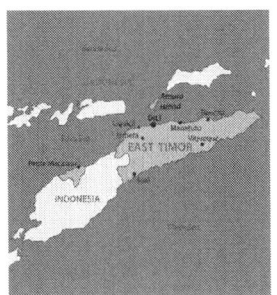

"Welcome home, Mr. President."

EAST TIMOR, FORMALLY KNOWN AS Portuguese Timor, is a small and impoverished country that shares the island of Java with Indonesia. For over four centuries it had been a Portuguese colony but in late 1975 it declared, and achieved, its independence from Portugal. The celebrations, however, were short-lived. That same year its larger neighbor to the west, Indonesia, fearing the establishment of a communist state, occupied it militarily and annexed it as its 27th province. From 1975 until 1999 an East Timorese guerrilla force fought a bloody campaign against the Indonesian forces. The leader of the resistance, who had for many years peacefully protested against Portugal's continued colonization of his land, became the face of the movement. He played a key role in alerting the world about the massacre in Dili, which occurred in 1991. This action made him public enemy number one in the eyes of the Indonesian government. As a result he was subsequently arrested, tried, convicted, and sentenced to life imprisonment. Like South Africa's Nelson Mandela, he successfully led the resistance from within prison and was eventually released in 1999. During the time of his imprisonment United Nations (UN) officials and other world dignitaries frequently visited him.

The resignation of the Indonesian President in May 1998 allowed for a UN-brokered agreement between Indonesia and Portugal. This opened the way for that international body to supervise a popular referendum that took place in August 1999. Despite a clear vote for independence the violence continued and an Australian-led international peacekeeping force was deployed until order was restored later that same year.

Macao was then still a Portuguese colony, and would remain so until the handover to China on December 20, 1999. With Portugal's direct involvement in East Timor's future, the Portuguese government enlisted our Chairman's assistance in providing the use of his business jet. That is how on December 14, 1999, we departed Macao aboard CS-XYZ, a Challenger CL601-3R, on a five-hour trip to Dili, East Timor's capital. Our lone passenger was a representative of the Macao government and a close friend of our Chairman. It was an exploratory trip for the purpose of assessing the conditions on the ground in preparation for another trip scheduled for a few days later. East Timor was still under the protection of UN peacekeepers due to sporadic violence still breaking out in various parts of the territory. Due to the high risk involved the plan was for us to land and wait by the aircraft for three hours before returning to Macao with the same passenger. The airport looked like a military base in times of war. There were guard towers, high fences with barbed wire, armored personnel carriers, UN peacekeepers on patrol wearing their blue helmets, and several military transport aircraft. In comparison our shining Challenger 601 business jet, with its sharply dressed pilots in civilian uniforms, looked completely out of place. Our brief stay, subsequent departure, and return flight to Macao were uneventful.

On December 18, 1999, we departed Macao once again for Dili. In addition to the same Macao government official we had before there was someone else on board whom I recognized from the news on TV. It was none other than the recently released and future President of East Timor. The trip was uneventful and after landing in Dili and opening the cabin door I extended my hand, shook his, and said, "Welcome home, Mr. President." He thanked me profusely and went down the stairs to step on a land that he had not seen in 23 years and for which he had sacrificed everything. After he disembarked he went around the crowded ramp and shook hands and posed for pictures with every UN peacekeeper there was…and there were a lot of them. There was something about him that left an indelible impression on me. He was very humble, kind, and grateful. There was no doubt you were in the presence of a statesman. Despite the many years he had spent locked behind bars, he did not display any hatred or animosity towards Indonesia. In fact, he quickly began a campaign of national reconciliation, nation building, and improved diplomatic relations with Indonesia.

East Timor remained under UN administration until May 20, 2002 when it became the first new sovereign state of the twenty first century. I am proud to have witnessed the birth of this new nation as well as to have had the privilege of meeting the man who was destined to become its first President, Xanana Gusmão. The following words describe his vision and mission for his nation:

"I believe that when people have an occupation that allows them to provide for their families, the social dimension of human nature will emerge instinctively and lead people to help and organize others less privileged."

It's a simple, but significant message. Any man who can so clearly express such wisdom, and then backs up those words with action, deserves an honorary place in my book.

27

"Captain, where would you recommend we go?"

ONE AFTERNOON I RECEIVED A call from Roger Lewis informing me that I would be taking his place as Captain on a 10-day trip to Europe that we had been originally scheduled to fly together starting the following day. On board would be our Chairman and some family members. He had been doing these biannual trips to Europe for some time and knew the routine pretty well. With me now flying as Captain I would be the one managing all aspects of the trip. That included dealing with the Chairman who at the time was in his mid 80s and did not like to waste time sitting in an airplane, whether on the ground or in-flight, for a minute longer than absolutely necessary. I understood and appreciated that when we reach a certain age every passing minute becomes even more precious. These trips to Europe were always very demanding and success depended on careful planning, precise execution, thinking ahead at all times, and being able to anticipate and promptly cope with sudden changes. I knew I was going to be under a magnifying glass but I took it as a challenge. My goal would be to give back to the Chairman every possible extra minute of his life by minimizing travel time, both in the air and on the ground.

The original plan had been to depart Hong Kong for Dubai where we would spend the night. Because of aircraft range limitations a fuel stop in Bombay, India, was required and planned. The following day we would depart Dubai for Cascais, Portugal, with another fuel stop in Larnaca, Cyprus, and a three-hour stopover for lunch in Madrid, Spain. After five days in Cascais we would fly to Paris, France, and spend three days in the "City of Lights" before embarking on the return trip to Hong Kong with an overnight in Dubai. Every detail of the trip had been reviewed, considered, planned, confirmed, and checked twice. We were ready to go.

The next day we departed with a crew of three and our four passengers on board B-XYZ, a Challenger 601-3R, which had been previously registered as CS-XYZ. The six hour and thirty-five minute trip to Bombay would take us through Southern China, Northern Myanmar, Dhaka, and across India to Bombay. Once we reached our cruise altitude and completed the Cruise checklist I got up from my seat to go to the lavatory. On the way back to the cockpit I informed the Chairman that the flight time from Hong Kong to Bombay would be six hours and thirty five minutes, that we would have a one-hour fuel stop in Bombay, and that the flight time from Bombay to Dubai would be two hours and forty five minutes. Unbeknown to me the Chairman had been doing a little math in his head and had already added all the times that I provided. So when he said, "Oh, so we will arrive in Dubai in ten hours and twenty minutes," I had to quickly make a mental calculation before I answered, "That's correct." Despite his advanced age, our Chairman had a very quick and sharp mind. I suddenly realized that I would have to be better prepared next time. Time to head back to the cockpit.

I knew that it was critical to minimize the duration of the fuel stop in Bombay so I called the ground handling agent on the satellite phone and emphasized the importance of expediting our arrival/departure procedures, including having the fuel truck standing by, lavatory and potable water equipment ready, and all paperwork duly completed. My First Officer loaded the second flight plan in the Flight Management System (FMS) and together we reviewed and briefed the arrival and subsequent departure procedures. After landing I met the ground handling agent and gave him a U.S. $100 bill with instructions to please distribute it among his dozen or so assistants. That tip may not seem like a lot of money in some countries but I knew his assistants would be grateful. I also informed him that for our return trip in ten days I would provide him and his assistants another U.S. $100 tip. Everything worked out perfectly and this was the quickest, and most efficient, fuel stop that I had ever experienced. A total of 35 minutes had elapsed from the moment we landed until the moment we were airborne again. For India, where we often encountered extensive red tape and inefficiency at its airports, that must have been a record. We were at least 25 minutes ahead of the game. Fortunately we had a very similar experience on our return trip.

The trip to Dubai was uneventful. There were no arrival delays and we landed about 30 minutes earlier than originally scheduled. Arrival procedures were completed with extraordinary efficiency and the Chairman and his family boarded a limousine in less than 20 minutes from the moment we opened the main cabin door. My crew and I still had to complete post-flight inspection and refueling procedures so it was another one and a half hours before we boarded a luxury van and headed out to our hotel. The first day of the trip had gone remarkably well and we had given the Chairman thirty minutes of his life back. To an old billionaire those precious minutes were worth more than money could buy. But there was no time to waste celebrating that day's accomplishments as we were barely getting started. It was time to get a good night sleep so as to be well rested for next day's grueling trip.

The following day we departed Dubai for the three and a half hour trip to Larnaca in the Mediterranean Sea. The trip took us across Saudi Arabia, Syria, Lebanon, and into Larnaca. The trip itself, and the subsequent fuel stop, were not only uneventful but we were actually fifteen minutes ahead of schedule. During the fuel stop in Larnaca the Chairman stepped out of the aircraft to stretch his legs. The refueling process was so quick that I found myself rushing the Chairman to get back into the aircraft so we could get going. How ironic it felt for me to be rushing him, as opposed to the other way around. I enjoyed the irony. Within 15 minutes of closing the main door we were airborne and on our way to Madrid. Once we leveled off at our cruise altitude for the five-hour trip, the Flight Attendant came to the cockpit and said, "Ivan, the Chairman would like to ask you a question and was wondering whether you could go back to the cabin." I said that I would be there shortly…as I pondered what this was all about.

When I got back to the cabin I found the Chairman sitting in his chair with a World Atlas on his lap looking at a map of Europe. I greeted him, sat across from him, and with the deference due to him I asked, "What can I do for you, Sir?" His answer, or rather, his question blew me away. Pointing at the map he asked, "Captain, where would you recommend we go?" I quickly realized that our well-planned and scheduled ten-day trip was about to change. Furthermore, I realized that we would most likely be going to whatever place I recommended so I had to think for a moment and be certain before I answered. "Italy. It's a beautiful country," I said. "Have you ever been to Capri?" I asked. He said that he had not been there and seemed happy for a little change in the routine. So he informed me that after departing Cascais we would spend two nights in Capri and one night in Paris. As I walked back to the cockpit and took my seat, I could only hope that he, his wife, and their kids would like Capri.

Capri is a very picturesque island located on the south side of the Gulf of Naples. It is surrounded by turquoise colored seas, has large green fields covered with flowers in an array of bright colors, and beautiful little towns nestled on the side of steep hills. It is a popular destination where the rich and famous go in their yachts and sailboats. What is there not to like, right? The closest airport is Naples so I made arrangements to have a helicopter pick up the Chairman and his family at the Naples airport and fly them to Capri. The twenty-minute flight would allow them to enjoy the sights of this gorgeous little island from the air.

The trip to, and brief stay in, Madrid was uneventful and we were soon heading to our final destination for the day, the charming little town of Cascais, north of Lisbon. Day two had gone remarkably well and we had given back to the Chairman more precious minutes of his life. For our stay in Cascais we had booked three rooms at one of the Chairman's best hotels in Portugal and my preferred choice while in Cascais, the Seaview do Guincho. This exclusive hotel has eighteen suites, a six-star French restaurant, and occupies the site of an old fort at the top of a cliff overlooking the Atlantic Ocean. It was absolutely gorgeous. The view from the rooms, of the beach and the sea, was breathtaking. I would often leave my window open so that I could hear the constant rhythm of the waves as they came up to and retreated from the rocky shore. At the lobby I would sit on a comfortable leather chair by the fireplace and savor a deliciously made cappuccino while enjoying the ocean view or reading a book. I also took strolls along the beach and enjoyed breathing the crisp, clean and cool breeze. All was going stupendously well until our Flight Attendant came over one day and complained to us that the hotel, while beautiful, comfortable, and luxurious, was simply too far away from the shopping area and restaurants. As someone from a big city, she wanted to be within walking distance of everything and everyone. So we reached a compromise with her. We would spend two nights at our current palace and the rest of the time we would stay at a hotel of her choice. She selected another one of the Chairman's hotels. This particular hotel was near another one of the Chairman's properties, The Grand Star Casino, one of Europe's largest casinos. There were dozens of restaurants and shops everywhere and she was absolutely delighted to be surrounded, once again, by large crowds, city lights, noise, pollution, cars honking their horns, and traffic jams. It felt as if we were back in Hong Kong!

The trip from Cascais to Naples was uneventful and pleasant. We taxied the aircraft to our designated parking stand and a Bell 206L LongRanger helicopter was standing by ready for our passengers to board. Within minutes, on what was a clear and sunny day, they were airborne and bound for Capri. After completing the post-flight inspection procedures and servicing the lavatory and potable water systems, we proceeded to our hotel. Within minutes of checking in and settling down in my hotel room I received a call from our Flight Attendant informing me, "Ivan, I just received a call from our passengers. The Chairman liked Capri very much but his family did not. Apparently Capri doesn't have large shopping areas and they want to go to Paris tomorrow morning. Can you organize it?" The following day the same helicopter picked them up by their hotel and brought them back to Naples where they boarded our aircraft so that we could fly them to Paris. Once in Paris the shopping spree began in earnest!

The rest of the trip went remarkably well and we completed each traveling day in record time giving the Chairman the extra minutes he cherished so much. My days as a trip advisor, however, were over. Nonetheless, upon our arrival in Hong Kong, the Chairman turned to me and very sternly said, "You did good." As I pointed to my crew, I replied, "Thank you, Mr. Chairman, but it was all three of us who did good."

From that point forward, requests from the Chairman's office for new trips would quote him as saying, "I want the pilot with the Italian last name." The Chairman had been shopping for precious extra minutes and my crew and I had given them to him. Despite Capri, the trip had been a complete success.

28

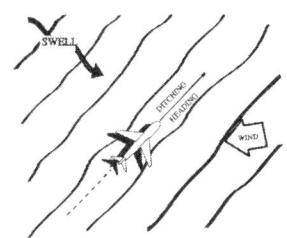

"Do you smell fumes?"

ONE OF THE MAIN REASONS I joined Jet ExecuAir in Macao in 1999 was because I needed a change. My previous job with BizJet Services in Singapore had consisted primarily of flying air ambulance missions to some of the most remote locations in the region. Because of the nature of air ambulance operations these trips were unusually demanding and riskier than traditional corporate flights. Upon completion of every one of those trips I had an enormous sense of professional pride and personal satisfaction. After all, we had completed them safely, effectively, and efficiently…and just as importantly, we had done something to help another human being. However, after nearly four years at BizJet Services, I was ready for a change. That much needed change came about when a position as a

Challenger Captain was offered to me.

This new position gave me the chance to fly larger and more advanced corporate jets with some very interesting passengers, as well as a chance to visit exotic destinations. My trips were now taking me to some of the most beautiful and far flung cities in Europe, Australia, Asia, and North America. In addition to flying the Chairman, his family and friends, we also flew numerous charters. Some of our charter clients included ex-U.S. Presidents, U.S. Senators, Ambassadors, ex-Prime Ministers, a member of a European Royal family, Hollywood celebrities, pop and opera singers, as well as CEOs and other high level executives from Fortune 500 companies.

One day we received a request to fly a charter to San Francisco, California. This was a somewhat unusual request as our charter trips were fairly regional but even more so because it was an air ambulance mission. Due to the distances involved, and the length of the duty period, two fuel stops and a complete change of crew would be required. Having thought that my days flying air ambulance trips were over, I found myself crewing the first portion of yet another such trip. The plan was to depart Hong Kong with the medical team, the patient and his family and fly them to San Francisco with fuel stops planned in Sapporo, Japan, and Anchorage, Alaska. A fresh crew would take over from us in Anchorage and continue on to San Francisco. Upon passenger drop-off and an overnight in San Francisco that crew would then return to Anchorage. We would then take over and continue the trip back to Macao with a fuel stop in Sapporo.

The Challenger 601 is not a suitable aircraft for air ambulance trips. Although it is spacious, quiet, and fast, and has a nearly 3,000-mile range, it would require lifting and carrying a heavy patient on a seven-foot long stretcher up the cabin stairs and into the cabin. Even if you somehow manage to do that you would still need to turn the stretcher and get it past a narrow wood-paneled entryway, through the cabin, and over delicate wood-veneered tables and leather-upholstered chairs. It would simply be too difficult, dangerous for the patient, and potentially cause too much damage to the expensive airplane interior. After explaining these difficulties and initially turning down the charter request we were assured by the medical team that this patient was in good enough medical condition to actually walk up the stairs, down the aisle, and then lay down on the sofa by himself. After departure the sofa could be extended into the aisle and turned into a bed with the patient safely secured utilizing specially designed seat belts. With the medical team's assurances with regards to the patient the trip was scheduled with B-XYB, a Challenger 601-3A, with a crew of three.

The first six-hour sector to Sapporo was uneventful. With typical Japanese efficiency once we were on the ground we managed to complete the refueling and arrival/departure procedures very quickly. Within 45 minutes we were airborne again flying eastbound into a cold winter night over the North Pacific Ocean. As we were climbing to our initial cruise altitude of FL370 (37,000 feet) we noted that the Traffic Collision and Avoidance System (TCAS) was displaying an intermittent red fail flag. There was not much we could do other than to switch it off, wait for a few minutes before turning it back on, and see if the fault would reset. When we turned it back on the TCAS unit functioned properly but I made a mental note to have an avionics technician look at it in San Francisco. We reached our cruise altitude, accelerated to Mach 0.80, completed the Cruise checklist, and noted that the initial fuel/time flight plan checks confirmed that all was progressing in accordance to the Operational Flight Plan. It was a smooth and beautiful night with a full moon and good weather forecast for our arrival into Anchorage.

The first indication that something wasn't right was the smell of burning wire. No visible smoke, no discernible heat source, just a strong smell from something that appeared to be electrical fumes. "Do you smell fumes?" I asked my First Officer. "I certainly do," he answered. Other than a now steady failure of the TCAS display, as indicated by a red flag, everything else in the cockpit appeared absolutely normal. We summoned the Flight Attendant to the cockpit, told her about the smell, asked her to check the galley and the cabin, and to report back to us. The galley, with its numerous electrical appliances, was the most likely source of the fumes. While she searched we donned our oxygen masks and kept looking for any indications of a fire. There were none that we could see. She returned and indicated that, although she could smell an unusual odor, everything was fine in the back. As good as that may sound there is nothing worse than a hidden fire so I asked her to check again. Upon her return she said she could smell something in a cabinet located across from the galley and right behind the cockpit. There was no smoke and no heat but when she removed the contents of the cabinet she noticed that there was a black metal box hidden behind in the space between the storage cabinet and the side wall next to it.

As a pilot there is nothing that scares me more than a cabin fire. Throw any type of emergency at me, but if you really want to see me sweat, light up a fire somewhere in the cabin. On countless occasions over the years I have taught Safety Equipment and Emergency Procedures (SEP) training to pilots and Flight Attendants. To emphasize how deadly serious a cabin fire is I would state, "There is nothing more potentially deadly than a cabin fire. A cabin fire will double in size every 20 to 25 seconds. You have two minutes to retrieve an extinguisher, find the fire, fight it, and put it out. If you fail to do so, you now have less than thirteen minutes to land and evacuate your passengers or ditch the aircraft and get your passengers into a raft before you lose total control of the aircraft." Once I got their attention with the previous statement I would continue by saying, "You can't call 911, evacuate via the closest emergency exit door, and let the fire fighters deal with the burning building. YOU are the fire fighters…and everyone's lives, including your own, depend on YOU. To successfully fight and survive a cabin fire the Flight Attendant must use aggressive and immediate action while the flight crew simultaneously points the aircraft to the nearest available runway, lands, and then carries out an evacuation." It is that serious, period.

So here we were. Sapporo was two hours behind us, Petropavlovsk, Russia, two hours ahead and the cold and dark

Pacific Ocean directly below us. When we had first noticed the fumes the thought occurred to me that if we had a hidden fire and couldn't find it in time and put it out within two minutes, we would have less than thirteen minutes to complete an emergency descent from FL370 and successfully ditch the aircraft at night before we lost control of the aircraft. We would then have had to get all passengers, including our 250-pound patient, out of the aircraft and into the life rafts. I felt a sense of dread at the thought but I knew full well that it was exactly what would have needed to be done. However, with no sign of smoke or fire anywhere in the galley area, lavatory or passenger cabin, plus the electrical burning smell now completely gone, we relaxed a bit. I decided to go back and check out the mystery black metal box the Flight Attendant had located earlier. This particular storage cabinet is used by the Flight Attendants to store all kinds of galley and cabin supplies so it is usually packed. Unbeknown to us until just a few minutes earlier, there was indeed a metal black box hidden behind the cabinet. There was still a barely perceivable trace of electrical fire smell emanating from the metal box. I felt confident we had located the source and that there had never been an actual cabin fire. Whatever had burnt had happened inside the box. I returned to the cockpit and discussed my findings with the First Officer who was still donning his oxygen mask.

The mystery was finally solved when we called our Engineering and Maintenance Department on the satellite phone and explained everything that had transpired. After studying the wiring diagrams the engineer was able to determine that the black metal box was the TCAS computer that had been installed some years earlier. The location was unusual and chosen simply because there had not been any available space in the avionics compartment located underneath the galley floor. The intermittent failure indications we had seen earlier in the TCAS instrument preceded the eventual and complete failure of the TCAS computer. Something inside the box caused electrical components to burn – and this resulted in the electrical fire smell we had detected. The engineer then asked that we remove electrical power to the TCAS box by pulling, and collaring, the corresponding circuit breaker. He then advised that arrangements to replace the damaged TCAS computer would be made in San Francisco.

We continued on to Anchorage and the rest of the trip was uneventful. Nonetheless we kept an open eye for any signs of trouble but fortunately there were none. Unlike the alarming smell of electrical fire we had noted earlier the cappuccino the Flight Attendant brought to me emitted the most pleasant aroma. Not only did I enjoy every sip of it but I now had a much greater appreciation for the importance of our sense of smell.

29

"Welcome aboard, Your Royal Highness."

A CHARTER BROKER FRIEND OF mine called me one day and said, "Ivan, I have a very important client who needs a business jet for a multiple-city, three-country, seven-day trip. I want you to be the Captain." The client he referred to was a member of a prominent Royal family and fourth in line to the throne at the time. As a member of the Royal family one of his many roles included being a Goodwill Ambassador and promoter of his country's products. He was scheduled to arrive in Singapore from Europe via the airlines. Starting in Singapore the trip would take us to Brunei, then Kota Kinabalu and Kuala Lumpur in Malaysia, and finally Batuan, Manila, and Panan-awan in the Philippines. After familiarizing ourselves with the royal protocol we departed Macao aboard

B-XYZ, a Challenger 601-3R, bound for Singapore to pick up the Prince and his entourage in what promised to be a challenging and interesting trip.

As we waited at Singapore's Changi airport ready for departure we did not really know what to expect of the Prince. I was standing by the foot of the stairs when he arrived and I said, "Welcome aboard, Your Royal Highness." He did not even notice me as he went up the stairs and into the cabin. As I was waving goodbye to the ground handling agent, and about to go up the stairs and into the cabin, the Prince came down running, shook my hand, and said, "Sorry about that Skipper. I didn't know you were down here." It was then I realized the Prince was comfortable dispensing with some of the protocol. Over the next few days he proved to be very down-to-earth, very conversational, and seemed like a genuinely good guy. The fact he was also a pilot, albeit a military helicopter pilot, made him easy to talk to. And so it began, the first of two Asian tours I flew with the Prince within six months.

There were times in flight when the Prince spent most of his time chatting with us in the cockpit. Being a pilot himself he was very curious about our Challenger 601 and asked lots of technical questions. He also wanted to enjoy the scenery as seen from the cockpit, especially when approaching the airport for landing. At one point I had to tell the Prince, "Your Highness, we are about to land. Would you please return to your seat and fasten your seat belt?" He graciously complied. At every airport we landed there would be a large welcoming party waiting to greet him...Honor Guard standing at attention, music band playing, and a long, rolled-out red carpet. I suspect they did not have many of these formal visits because the ground crew often seemed to miscalculate where to stop the aircraft. After landing we would taxi the aircraft to a designated location at the airport and then follow the marshaller's instructions to the parking stand so as to stop the aircraft in such a way that, when the main cabin door was opened, the red carpet would be directly in front of it. At one point I noted from the cockpit, with horror, how the Prince, upon exiting the aircraft, had to turn and walk several feet towards the red carpet before he could walk on it. It was embarrassing but neither the Prince nor his entourage made a fuss about it. This was another indication the Prince, despite his position, was a reasonable and down-to-earth individual.

Most of the airports we visited had the infrastructure necessary to handle business jets. However there was one airport in particular that totally lacked the basic ground support services required to assist us. This was evident when we asked for potable water to service the aircraft's water system – a very standard request. They said, "Sorry, we just don't have that type of equipment." Then, we asked them to service the lavatory. Again, another very standard request. They said, "Sorry, we don't have that type of equipment either." The lavatory needed servicing and the last thing that we wanted was for it to smell. So, my co-Captain and I considered our options…or shall I say, our only option. We would have to service it ourselves without the usual unit that connects to the aircraft, drains its contents, and refills it with clean water. Using a pair of 20-gallon plastic bags we carefully and tightly wrapped them around the 3-inch nozzle. When that was done one of us pulled the release handle. The 8-10 liters of waste came rushing down the nozzle fast and, fortunately, into the plastic double bags. Disposing of the bags wasn't a problem as the ground handling agent was happy to take them away from us. We then asked for a bucket with clean water so that we could pour it directly into the toilet and he said, "Sorry, we don't have any buckets either." There was just one thing we could do. In the baggage compartment we had a couple of boxes of one-liter Evian bottles. We ended up pouring water out of seven of these bottles into the toilet. That must have been the first time ever a business jet toilet had been serviced to flush with Evian water. I suspect not even Buckingham Palace offers such luxurious treatment to its tenants and distinguished visitors!

The rest of the trip was uneventful and the Prince returned to his country having successfully accomplished his Goodwill Ambassador work. A few months later we met again for another challenging multiple-city, multiple-country, and multiple-day trip. As for the airport in question we've renamed it the Royal Evian International Airport in memory of the occasion. Fortunately I have never been back nor have I ever had to use plastic bags in that manner again. I am just happy to say, "Been there, done that, bought the t-shirt," and we even managed, miraculously, not to splash any waste all over us!

Flying an aircraft safely from point A to point B is the most important aspect of what we do. That is a given and we take that part of our job very seriously. You could even say that is the reason why we get paid the big bucks. As corporate pilots, however, we do much more than just flying. We do whatever can be done, safely and legally, to get the job done. Even if that means putting your Rolex watch in your pocket and rolling up your sleeves so that you can vacuum the carpet or even service the aircraft's lavatory and potable water systems. These tasks are normally carried out by companies subcontracted to perform them. However, in a rare situation such as the one described before we are fully prepared to do it ourselves. Such is the nature of corporate aviation.

30

Encounter with an angry ghost

DURING THE FOUR YEARS I lived in Singapore I made quite a few friends so whenever I had a trip to that beautiful country I would make it a point to see them. That was the case when my crew and I departed from Hong Kong with three passengers and arrived at Singapore's Seletar airport for a three-day stay. On this particular occasion hotel reservations had been made at the Bellevue hotel conveniently located near the famous Orchard Road. I had previously agreed to meet with a good friend of mine in the lobby of the hotel a short time after our arrival but when we got there at around 10 PM he was already waiting in the lobby. We greeted each other and agreed to meet at the hotel bar for a drink fifteen minutes later. That would give me enough time to check in and drop off my luggage in the room.

Our Dispatch office had booked the three rooms for my crew and me under my name. This was convenient because they only had to make a single reservation as opposed to three separate ones. Upon check in we would each present our respective passports and company credit cards and, in the case of my fellow crewmembers, register using their own names. Knowing that my friend was waiting for me at the bar and that he had already been waiting for a long time I took the elevator to my floor and quickly walked across the long corridor to my room. Once inside I opened my suitcase, retrieved a pair of jeans, a polo shirt, a pair of loafers, and promptly changed out of my pilot's uniform. Right after I left the room and started walking towards the elevators I suddenly realized that, in my haste, I had forgotten my room key. So I made a mental note to stop by the front desk to ask for a new one before returning to the room later that night.

My friend and I spent the next two hours or so reminiscing about good old times while enjoying a few icy cold beers and a few snacks. By the time we decided to call it a night I was already feeling quite tired and slightly drunk. Fortunately I wasn't drunk enough to forget to stop by the front desk on my way back to the room and request a new key. So I said, "I am afraid I left my key inside my room. Would you please provide me with a new one?" To which the front desk attendant very politely asked me, "May I please have your room number?" That's when I realized that not only had I forgotten my room key, I had not even paid enough attention to the room number to remember it. So I said, "I don't remember, but my name is Ivan Luciani and I just checked in earlier tonight." Again, very politely and patiently, he asked, "May I please see some form of identification?" Fortunately I had my wallet with me so I presented my ID card. Although I wasn't able to produce my passport he seemed satisfied with the ID card and that I was who I said I was. So he provided me a new room key, advised me which room number I was in, and wished me a good night. A peculiar aspect of the Bellevue hotel is that the elevators to the new wing are a fair distance from the lobby. Furthermore the corridors are very long so I had to walk quite a distance to my room. When I finally got there I inserted my newly issued key into the door lock and, except for a steady red light on the lock, absolutely nothing happened. Two more attempts produced the same result so I had no choice but to walk back along the long corridor to the elevators, patiently wait for one to arrive, go down to the lobby, and then walk the long distance to the front desk. The same gentleman who had previously handed me the key looked at me with surprise and asked me, "Is everything OK, Mr. Luciani?" "Not OK, the room key you gave me does not work," I said. He apologized profusely, confirmed in the computer that he had the correct room number, and as a precaution, programmed and gave me two new room keys. "Here you go, Sir. My apologies once again. Goodnight, Mr. Luciani." After a quick "Thank you," I turned around and walked back across the lobby all the way to where the elevators were, patiently waited for the next one to open, went back up to my floor, walked again along the long corridor to my room, inserted the room key in the door lock...and was rudely welcomed by a steady red light! Not wanting to go back to the lobby I desperately tried both keys several times...and had the same result. "Damn it," I said. I was very tired, felt quite sleepy, was a bit drunk...and my patience was getting thin. So, I walked back along the long corridor to the elevators, got in the next one and went down, walked towards the lobby and saw the same gentleman behind the front desk. By then I was feeling quite irritated so before he could even say a word I drily said, "Neither one of these two keys worked!" The person next to him realized the predicament his colleague was in and promptly offered to assist. Within a few seconds I received more apologies and yet another pair of room keys. So feeling quite frustrated I said, "If these keys don't work you are coming with me to unlock the door." Then I turned around, walked across the lobby all the way to the elevators, got in and went up to my floor, walked all the way down the long corridor to my room, inserted the key...and, to my astonishment, I saw the same steady red light. What happened next nearly gave me a heart attack!

The door swung open and a horrible ghost with a twisted face yelled at me "IVAN, THIS IS NOT YOUR ROOM!" I have never believed in ghosts but there was definitely one standing in my room that night and apparently it even knew my name. From the shock I found myself unable to breathe or move. In fact I think I nearly peed my pants! The ghost must have realized the effect it had had on me because, in a soothing voice, it gently asked, "Ivan, are you OK?" After a few seconds I started to breathe again but felt my heart pumping so fast that I thought it was going to come out of my chest. Then the figure of this angry ghost started to slowly take shape and I realized that it wasn't a ghost after all but my annoyed Flight Attendant. She was wearing a long and wrinkled white gown, a white shower cap over her hair, and some sort of white cream or powder all over her face. With the room lights off she really did look like a ghost. It turns out she had heard my repeated attempts to open the door over the previous 45 minutes but, because she had locked the door from the inside, the keys I had received did not work. In any case she had had enough and decided to open the door and let me know that I was trying to enter the wrong room.

After realizing what had happened I felt incredibly embarrassed and apologized to her profusely. She accepted my apologies and wished me a good night. So I headed back towards the elevators via the long corridor, waited for the next elevator, got in and went down, and then walked all the way back to the front desk. The surprised look on the faces of the gentlemen behind the desk prompted me to quickly say, "That room belongs to my colleague." It took just a few seconds for them to check the computer and realize that my Flight Attendant's room was still listed under my name. Within a few more seconds they changed my name for hers and determined that there was just one more room under my name. With the mystery solved they handed me a couple of keys to the correct room. So, for the fourth time that evening I turned around, walked all the way to the elevators, waited for the next one to arrive, got in and went up to my floor, then walked along the very familiar long corridor all the way to the correct room, inserted the new key with some trepidation…and was welcomed by a steady green light. It had taken nearly an hour before I had finally arrived back at my room and a nice bed. By then I was simply too tired and sleepy to get undressed so I just collapsed on the bed and did not wake up until several hours later…feeling dehydrated and still quite embarrassed about the whole episode.

It's been a few years since that episode but my Flight Attendant and I still laugh about it. Fortunately she did not take offense at being mistaken for not just a ghost, but an angry one. For some unknown reason we never booked rooms at the Bellevue hotel again. That was fine by me as there was way too much walking required just to get to your room. As for me, I made it a point to always ensure my room key was in my wallet before I walked out of the room and I paid particular attention to the room number. These precautions have spared me a great deal of aggravation. Besides, just because I don't believe in ghosts does not mean I want to ever take a chance of having an encounter with another one. A single encounter with an angry ghost has been enough for me!

31

"Chelsie, guess who I am going to fly?"

LIKE MOST PEOPLE, I ENJOY going to the movies and watching a great movie. Hollywood sure knows how to keep us entertained, and hooked, with excellent movies – whether action, drama, suspense or comedy. I have seen so many great movies over the years that I stopped having a single favorite a long time ago. When it comes to actors, however, there are just a handful of them I really like. Among them is one particular actor I consider the best action actor of his era.

You can imagine my surprise to learn I would be flying him on a three-day tour of several Asian cities during the promotion of the second installment of his latest blockbuster movie. The plan was to pick him up in Hong Kong and fly him to Taipei, then to Seoul, and finally to Tokyo (Narita) where he would catch a commercial flight back to the U.S. To my teenage daughter I said, "Chelsie, guess who I am going to fly?" "Who?" she obliged. When I told her I was surprised by her complete lack of reaction or even verbal response. She didn't even flinch and actually looked bored. Still hoping for some sort of response I quickly mentioned one of his best movies, one I knew she had definitely seen. What she said next totally blew me away. Somewhat annoyed she responded, "Come on, Dad. It's not as if he is Harrison Ford." Wow – not the answer I had expected…at all. After I recovered from the shock I just couldn't help but laugh. Well, she does have a good point. Harrison Ford is a phenomenal actor and another one of my favorites. Over the years I have seen many of his movies and it's hard to decide which one I like best. Still, it was interesting to learn that, unlike most other thirteen-year old girls, my daughter's idea of a cool actor was based exclusively on his acting skills, not just his good looks. Well, I will have to patiently wait for an opportunity to fly Harrison Ford someday just so that I may impress her.

The following week we departed Macao aboard B-XYZ, a Challenger 601-3R, bound for Hong Kong for the start of the tour. Our famous passenger had already been in Hong Kong for a few days promoting the movie, and was the talk of the town. He had been staying at the Peninsula Hotel, one of the most prestigious five-star hotels in Hong Kong, which with its rooftop heliport and fleet of modern twin-engine helicopters, allowed him to arrive at the airport by air in a matter of minutes. The short but scenic ride allowed him to avoid the large crowds camped outside the hotel. Nonetheless, the secret about his departure from Hong Kong was out because there were hundreds of fans gathered at the Business Aviation Center (BAC), a private jet terminal, hoping to catch a glimpse of the famous actor. There were also many paparazzi aiming their powerful cameras towards our aircraft. It was an eerie and unfamiliar feeling to have all eyes aimed at us...not to mention a huge distraction.

After landing we watched him get off the helicopter and, accompanied by the movie's director and a bodyguard, walk calmly and confidently towards our aircraft. Once on board, and before I could greet him, he extended his hand, firmly shook mine, and introduced himself. It was a strange feeling to see in person someone I had only seen on the big screen. After welcoming them I closed the cabin door, returned to the cockpit, strapped down, and made a conscious decision to forget who we had on board and to focus instead on the task at hand – flying. And so it began, a trip with an actor who, at the time, was likely the most popular movie star in Hollywood. Someone who attracts huge crowds wherever he went and, as we soon found out, that even included airport staff who were on duty. As soon as we landed and he got off the plane he was immediately surrounded by hundreds of airport workers. I kept asking myself, was anybody left working at the airport? He made it a point to graciously pose with the cheering crowds...despite what must have felt like a very chaotic scene.

Like Harrison Ford, this actor is also an aviation enthusiast and a pilot. He owns several airplanes, including a Gulfstream business jet that he flies under the supervision and guidance of an experienced professional pilot. So, it was not surprising when he asked, through the Flight Attendant, whether he could sit in the jump seat during the cruise phase of the flight (the workload is the lowest during this phase of flight). This is not an unusual request from passengers but it is up to the Captain to accept or decline such requests. My co-Captain and I looked at each other, nodded in agreement, and told the Flight Attendant that he was welcome to join us. As the Flight Attendant helped him strap down in the jump seat and put on the headset it dawned on me how weird it would feel to have this remarkable actor sitting right behind us. After thanking us for letting him sit in the jump seat the first thing he asked was, "What type of avionics do you have?" He was very interested in talking about aviation and seemed quite knowledgeable about it. I guess this was a break that provided him an escape from the rigors of promoting a movie, which is a lot of work I am sure. It also allowed him to engage in something that he loved – flying – but didn't get to enjoy as often. After the initial weirdness wore off we tried to keep the conversation relaxed and treated him as just another pilot. It turns out that he learned to fly near Vancouver, Canada, at an airport that my co-Captain used to fly from, so that resulted in another extended discussion. At one point he asked, "You guys want to ask me any questions about movies?" No, not really, I thought to myself. As I said earlier I do enjoy going to the movies to watch great movies but I personally don't really care a whole lot about what happens behind the scenes. Not wanting to come across as impolite or uninterested in his glamorous job I asked him, "How long does it take to make a movie?" He started to explain something along the lines of it taking several months and blah blah blah...so we quickly steered the conversation back to the world we were all passionate about, aviation. Yeah!

Unlike his action-packed movies our flights were smooth and easy. We did not buzz any control towers, engage in air-to-air combat with enemy fighter jets, fly upside down or attempt to land on an aircraft carrier in the middle of the night. In fact, the most dangerous thing we encountered were the hordes of screaming fans eager to see our passenger in the flesh. I also remember how, after our passengers had boarded, an airport worker came quickly on board, walked into the cabin and asked for an autograph. Our passenger had already posed for pictures with the airport workers outside the aircraft and had also signed autographs, so I thought it was highly inappropriate for this airport worker to just come on board without even asking for permission. I didn't see the bodyguard try to stop him, as I had expected him to do, so I didn't intervene. As soon as this airport worker got off the aircraft, autographed photo in one hand, camera on the other, and a satisfied smile on his face, I closed the cabin door. It was all very chaotic. "How does he stand this madness?" I asked myself as I returned to the cockpit. I guess that's the price actors/celebrities have to pay for being celebrities/famous.

It's been quite a few years since that memorable trip but I still remember his pleasant and relaxed demeanor. My favorite recollection of that trip, however, is that of three individuals, each with a passion for aviation, sharing a private moment to talk about airplanes...without much more being said about anything else. It just so happens that one of those three pilots sitting in that cockpit was also a Hollywood superstar. How cool was that? I am still waiting for the opportunity to fly Harrison Ford one of these days, just so that I can ask my now grown-up daughter, "Chelsie, guess who I am going to fly?" It would be great to meet him and to have him with us in the cockpit. As a passionate aviator himself I am sure he would love to exchange stories about aviation with two other equally passionate aviators.

I love my job!

32

VIP

"Quick, quick, we can go now!"

A LOT OF OUR CHARTER clients were high-level executives coming from either North America or Europe. These executives would normally travel via the airlines to a major Asian city where we would pick them up in one of our business jets. Typically, these charters would cover several cities and countries within just a few days. Once their business activities in Asia were complete they would then return home via the airlines. Their companies were large enough to probably own a fleet of business jets but I am sure some "bean counter" figured that it would be cheaper to charter a local jet than to fly theirs all the way from their respective countries. Whatever the rationale, we had a steady flow of charter clients for our business jets.

One such trip involved picking up four North American executives in Dhaka, Bangladesh, and flying them to seven cities in India and Sri Lanka within five days. Starting in Dhaka, these cities were Calcutta (now Kolkata), Bangalore (now Bengaluru) Coimbatore, Mumbai (formerly Bombay), Chandigarh, and New Delhi in India, and Colombo in Sri Lanka. A trip like this would be impossible to accomplish with the airlines. The flexibility that a business jet offers allows executives to complete their job safely and efficiently and in complete privacy and comfort. Nonetheless, this trip would be a lot of work for them and for us.

We departed Macao aboard B-XYB, a Challenger 601-3A, with a crew of three for what promised to be a very demanding trip. Operating business jets in and out of airports in that part of Asia was considered a character-building exercise because of the amount of red tape required to make anything happen. But, having already flown extensively in the area, I knew exactly what to expect. The arrival and departure formalities at these airports can be overwhelming and time-consuming. For each departure it would take us about 45 minutes to get from the main terminal to where the aircraft was. Once at the aircraft I would have to leave my crew to get the aircraft ready while I accompanied the ground handling agent to the various offices situated in different locations at the airport terminal. This process was required so that I could file the flight plan, get a verbal weather briefing plus a weather package, pay numerous invoices in cash at different offices, and get the General Declaration (GEN DEC), which lists all passengers and their details, stamped by no less than six government entities: customs, immigration, quarantine, airport authority, police, and the military. I must have signed half a dozen different forms and each one of them had to be stamped by someone seemingly employed exclusively for that purpose. The whole process was beyond ridiculous but, unfortunately, it is typical of the way their bureaucracy functioned. The term "red tape" has a completely new meaning in this region. None of this, however, prepared me for what happened at one of these airports.

After spending the night at a gorgeous hotel in a beautiful Indian city we were picked up by the designated driver three hours before the scheduled departure. This took into account an anticipated one-hour drive from the hotel to the airport. We arrived at the airport as planned, two hours before departure. Oddly enough, there were hundreds of people standing outside the terminal. When we met the ground handling agent by the curb and asked him what was going on he apologetically said, "Sorry but we have to wait outside the terminal. There is a VIP departure." We then asked, "Do you know how long we have to wait?" To which he replied, "Shouldn't be too long." We waited and waited and waited…and the longer we waited the more concerned we became. Finally, we put so much pressure on the poor agent that he went over to see what he could do to at least let us get to the aircraft and get it ready for our own departure. By then we had about an hour and a half to go and if it took much longer we would not be able to depart on time. Fifteen minutes later we saw our agent running towards us and, almost out of breath, he frantically said, "Quick, quick. We can go now. I just found out that YOU are the VIP!"

By then it was clear that not only were we going to be late

departing that day but that we had also been the reason why there were hundreds of people stranded outside the main terminal. How ironic and unfortunate that a well-intended effort from the local authorities to give our passengers the VIP treatment actually ended up delaying their departure…and, it seemed, everyone else's. Not surprisingly, while we were busy getting the aircraft refueled and ready for departure, our passengers arrived. I welcomed them and, without offering too many details, informed them that we would have a delayed departure. Regrettably, they had no choice but to patiently wait in the cabin until we completed the pre-flight inspection, the refueling procedure, and our pre-departure safety briefings. At the same time our Flight Attendant was busy receiving, organizing, and storing all the catering plus inspecting all the cabin safety equipment. The whole episode was most unfortunate as this wasn't the way business aviation was supposed to operate. Fortunately this was the only hiccup on the entire trip and, although it sounds kind of funny when we talk about it now, it most certainly wasn't at the time.

At the conclusion of this very demanding trip our exhausted executives boarded a commercial flight from Colombo bound for their home country. My crew and I, on the other hand, were able to spend the night at a nice hotel for some much needed rest. The following day we were picked up at the hotel, driven to the airport, and were pleased <u>not</u> to see hundreds of people stranded outside the terminal waiting for some VIP passengers to depart!

33

"Guys, I think we forgot the President's bag."

ONE OF THE JOYS OF business aviation is that every trip is different. There is just no routine in what we do. We travel to different cities around the world and get to see and do new things. At times you may find yourself having breakfast in Paris, lunch in Rome, and dinner in Moscow...all in the same day. That's the nature of the job. Another interesting aspect of the job is that we get to fly some fascinating individuals. I have flown Ambassadors, ex-Presidents, U.S. Senators, ex-Prime Ministers, members of royalty, Hollywood actors, famous singers, and many others. It was on one of those occasions that the Flight Attendant came up to the cockpit and said, "Guys, I think we forgot the President's bag."

Earlier that day we flew from Macao to Hong Kong to pick up a former U.S. President and fly him to Shanghai, China, where he had a speaking engagement. After dropping him off in Shanghai we were scheduled to return to our home base, Macao. The trip itself was not particularly significant in its duration and destination except for the obvious fact we had a former U.S President on board. He had just left office a couple of months earlier so instead of flying on board Air Force One, one of two highly modified Boeing 747 jumbo jets that had served his travel needs while in office, he was going to fly in a much humbler, 12-seat, Bombardier Challenger 601 business jet. Having previously flown a multiple-country trip in a similar aircraft with another former U.S. President I was looking forward to flying another such trip.

We flew to Hong Kong in B-XYB, a Challenger 601-3A, and after landing we taxied to the private jet terminal. At the parking stand we shut the engines down and started to prepare for our next departure which was scheduled for a couple of hours later. As the departure time neared we started to notice an increasing number of people gathering on the ramp. In addition to reporters and news cameramen most were people who worked at the private jet terminal and the various aircraft management companies that had their operations there. The secret, if it had been one, must have gotten out because there were hundreds of people hoping to catch a glimpse of the former and popular U.S. President.

The first thing that caught my attention after his arrival at the airport was that he shook everyone's hands regardless of how far they were from where he stood at the time. It's almost as if he made it a point to walk towards those people standing in the back just to make sure he did not miss the opportunity to shake their hands also. Considering how many people there were, and that he wasn't courting potential voters, this was an amazing gesture on his part. Shortly before he boarded some of the Secret Service agents came on board, introduced themselves, and handed over the baggage. This was followed shortly thereafter by the arrival of a member of the HK security services who handed a Secret Service agent a locked hard case, which contained their unloaded service weapons. "Skipper," the lead Secret Service agent said to me, "please store this case as you deem appropriate. I'll collect it from you after landing."

The President boarded, politely said "hi" to the crew, and took his seat. Engine start and taxi clearances were promptly received and we had an on-time departure for what would be a pleasant two-hour flight to Shanghai International Airport in Pudong, China. Upon landing we taxied to the designated ramp and parking stand and noted what must have been hundreds of people waiting to receive the President. "Welcome to Shanghai, Mr. President," I said. "Thank you, Captain. Would you like a picture?" he asked. He must have seen the surprise on my face because he said, "It's OK. Get us a camera." Although I had a camera nearby I had not intended to ever ask him to pose for a picture, but now that he had asked I grabbed it quickly. As soon as he saw the camera in my hand he snatched it and gave it to the nearest Secret Service agent. And so, the entire crew posed with the former

President at the foot of the stairs – with our humbler version of Air Force One in the background!

We then unloaded the baggage and started to get the aircraft ready for the return flight as the former President shook hands and posed for pictures with the members of the welcoming committee. Shortly thereafter he boarded a limo and we watched as the convoy of vehicles disappeared. It had been a short but memorable trip and it was time to head home. After receiving the appropriate air traffic control clearance we departed Shanghai and were climbing to our cruise altitude when the Flight Attendant came to the cockpit and solemnly announced, "Guys, I think we forgot the President's bag." My co-Captain and I looked at each other with surprise and then I asked her, "How do you know it is his bag?" To which she replied, "It's got a big seal on the front that says 'Seal of the President of the United States of America.' " So, resigned that we had indeed forgotten his bag, I said, "OK, that's good enough for me. We'll return to Shanghai." To my co-Captain, I said, "Call the office on the satellite phone, notify them that we are heading back to Shanghai, and ask them to contact the Secret Service. I'll talk to air traffic control."

Twenty minutes later we landed and taxied to the parking stand where a member of the former President's security detail awaited. Feeling quite embarrassed I handed the bag to an even more embarrassed Secret Service agent. We looked at each other for a few seconds and, with a smile, we said, "Goodbye…again." Nothing else needed to be said as we understood each other and were deeply grateful that the forgotten soft black leather bag with the golden seal had been promptly returned.

As we flew back to Macao it occurred to me that there was a good reason the famous nuclear "football" is cuffed to the wrist of the military officer responsible for carrying it. The briefcase, which contains authentication launch codes, is intended to be used by the President of the United States to authorize a nuclear attack or counterattack while away from fixed command centers. Being cuffed to the military officer trailing the President is probably the best way to ensure it is not accidentally left behind…like we did with this former President's personal briefcase.

After all of these years I am still embarrassed by it!

34

"Your landing permit has been revoked."

IN 2003 WE LEARNED A term we had never heard before and would never forget: SARS (Severe Acute Respiratory Syndrome). This rare and viral disease created havoc around the world because of its sudden and unknown origin, rapid spread, and lack of an available cure. It all began in November 2002 with the unexplained death of a farmer in the Chinese province of Guangdong in southern China.

Within a matter of months there were several thousand people infected in thirty seven countries in Asia, North America, Europe, and Africa. Before effective measures to control its spread were finally implemented, unsuspecting passengers had contracted the disease and were traveling by air, reaching distant and sometimes woefully unprepared countries. Compounding the problem even further was the fact that the flu-like symptoms would not show up for approximately ten days after a person became infected. Typical symptoms included fever, myalgia, lethargy, cough, sore throat, and other nonspecific symptoms. The only symptom common to all patients appeared to be a fever above 38°C (100°F). As a result, all inbound travelers had to be scanned for signs of high fever. Although SARS affected people of all ages the mortality rate was highest among the elderly and the young. By the time the epidemic was finally contained in January 2004 more than 800 of those infected had succumbed to it.

Most cases of SARS were concentrated in China and in Hong Kong with 5,328 and 1,755 cases respectively. Macao quickly implemented a number of measures to protect its citizens and prevent the spread of SARS. These measures consisted of early detection and isolation of suspected cases in designated quarantine areas of the hospitals. All border crossing points, the airport and heliport, and the ferry terminals were on alert. In addition, there was a public campaign that encouraged frequent handwashing, disinfection of surfaces, use of surgical masks, avoidance of contact with bodily fluids, etc. As a result of these measures there was only one documented case of SARS in Macao. This was a remarkable level of success. However, because of Macao's proximity with Guangdong and Hong Kong, our Chairman and a few family members elected to place some distance between themselves and the region. They promptly boarded a

Cathay Pacific flight to Perth, Australia, a country the virus had not reached yet and, fortunately, would not.

Sometime after our Chairman and his family arrived in Australia they requested one of our business jets for a trip to Europe. What was unusual about this request was that the Chairman wanted us to fly to Perth and then wait for ten days in order to confirm we had not developed the flu-like symptoms associated with SARS. Only then would he board the aircraft for the trip to Europe. A few days later we departed Macao with a crew of three aboard B-XYB, a Challenger 601-3A, bound for Perth with a fuel stop in Bali, Indonesia. The flights to Bali and Perth were both uneventful and upon arrival we settled in one of the Chairman's hotels for what seemed like a ten-day paid vacation in this beautiful city in western Australia.

An interesting fact about traveling to Australia is that this country has a unique requirement for the aircraft cockpit, passenger cabin, and baggage compartment to be sprayed with an approved insecticide. This task must be accomplished after the cabin door is closed at the foreign airport of departure as well as prior to commencing the descent in preparation for landing at the Australian airport. These measures prevent the inadvertent introduction of species that may harm their agricultural industry. After landing the flight crew is not permitted to open the cabin door until they have shown from the cockpit the two color-coded, empty aerosol cans to the agriculture officer meeting the aircraft (the green aerosol can is used specifically before departure while the blue one is used before descent). Only then do they receive a thumbs up from the officer to open the cabin door. The cans are then collected by the same officer who ensures that they are indeed empty before he disposes of them. In addition, all the food onboard is also bagged, collected, and disposed of. None of these measures, however, would have prevented the spread of SARS into the country.

After reassuring our Chairman that none of us had developed the flu-like symptoms over the previous ten days, and that we actually felt quite healthy, he decided to first fly to Sydney for a few days. He did make an additional and rather strange request. We were to wear face masks during the trip to Sydney as well as during the return trip to Perth. It felt really weird to wear a face mask while flying, particularly when you consider how long it takes to fly from one side of this vast country to the other, but it provided the Chairman with peace of mind so we were happy to oblige. During the flights to and from Sydney we used a black marker to draw open mouths with large teeth on our face masks. This gave us a good laugh and we snapped a few pictures of each other. Little did we know at the time that a few days later SARS would be having the last laugh.

The plan for the trip to Europe was to depart Perth with our Chairman and several passengers, land in the Maldives, and spend two nights. We would then depart the Maldives for Larnaca, Cyprus, with a fuel stop in Dubai. After three nights in Larnaca we would then depart for Cascais, Portugal, with a brief stop in Madrid, Spain, for lunch. After spending several days in Cascais we would then embark on the return trip to Hong Kong. That was the plan. It all changed suddenly when, while we were in-flight to Larnaca, the person on the other side of the satellite phone stated, "Your landing permit has been revoked." I will get to that later on.

The trip from Perth to the Maldives was long but uneventful and over the course of three days and two nights we enjoyed ourselves in this remarkable place. There were hardly any other visitors so we had the whole resort for ourselves. After three sun-filled days it was time to depart for Larnaca. We had used Larnaca as a fuel stop on numerous occasions in the past but this would be the first time we would actually have any chance to visit and explore it. We were all looking forward to it. The trip to Dubai, our fuel stop, was uneventful. As in previous occasions ground handling services provided by the local service provider were excellent and we managed a quick turnaround. Within forty five minutes we were airborne again for the final flight of the day to Larnaca.

One hour prior to landing I used the satellite phone to call the ground handling agent with the intention of advising our estimated time of arrival (ETA) and to request potable water and lavatory services. I quickly realized that something wasn't right when I detected some reluctance in her voice. At last she said, "Your landing permit has been revoked." A shiver went up my spine as I asked why. She said something to the effect that the landing authorization had just been revoked because we were a "Chinese aircraft and they are concerned with SARS." A million things were going through my head as I quickly evaluated options, none of which seemed good. So I said, "We are not a Chinese aircraft. We are a Macao-registered aircraft coming from Australia via the

Maldives and Dubai, and we intend to land in Larnaca." She seemed to hesitate and nervously said, "I don't know if they will let you land, but I will convey your message." I then proceeded to brief my co-Captain who, like me, was completely incredulous…and deeply concerned about this sudden turn of events. We then summoned the Flight Attendant to the cockpit and, after briefing her, asked her to explain to the Chairman the situation and our intentions. About forty five minutes prior to arrival, as we crossed the Syrian border into Cyprus, the Damascus air traffic controller handed us off to the Nicosia air traffic controller. We knew this would be it. My co-Captain keyed the microphone and checked in: "Nicosia Control, Bravo Xray Yankee Bravo (B-XYB), overhead NIKAS (our present position), Flight Level three niner zero (39,000 feet), squawk 3527," to which the controller simply said, "Bravo Xray Yankee Bravo, Nicosia Control, radar contact, advise ready for descent." That was music to our ears and we relaxed a bit. OK, so far so good. "Looks like they've established that we are not a Chinese aircraft and do not pose any health risk to them," I said. We then informed our Flight Attendant that everything appeared to be OK and that we would be commencing our descent in fifteen minutes.

The approach and landing were uneventful. We vacated the runway and followed the "follow me car" that guides aircraft to their designated parking stand. When we arrived at that spot and shut the engines down we noted that we were in the most remote location of the airport. It was obvious they were keeping us away from everything and everyone. I opened the main cabin door, deplaned, and proceeded to meet the "follow me car" driver. What he said next blew me away! He said, "You can refuel but you cannot stay here. We will not service your lavatory or potable water systems. You have to go as soon as the refueling is complete." All attempts to discuss who we were and where we came from were futile. I went back inside the aircraft and explained the situation to the Chairman. The bottom line was that the Cyprus authorities were deeply concerned about the SARS virus and saw us as a health threat. The Chairman disembarked and introduced himself to the driver but, regardless of how much he tried to explain to this individual who he was and that everyone had been outside of Asia for more than ten days, the answer was still the same, "You have to leave as soon as the refueling is complete." I watched in frustration as this eighty three year old billionaire and gentleman, whose vast business empire employed thousands of people worldwide and who rubbed shoulders with world leaders was trying, and failing, to have a rational discussion with this airport worker. He was being told, in no uncertain terms, that he had to leave. I escorted the Chairman back inside the cabin and then went to the cockpit to brief my co-Captain. I then asked him to prepare the aircraft for departure and to supervise the refueling. When he asked me, "Where are we going and how much fuel do we need?" I said, "I will call Houston (that's where our primary handling agent, Universal Weather and Aviation, is based) to see if they can get permits and prepare a flight plan to some European city. Fill up the tanks."

I called Universal (UV), explained our predicament, and asked which European country and city we could proceed to on such a short notice. The agent suggested Madrid and said that he could have a flight plan filed within the hour. "Okay," I said. "We'll go to Madrid. I will call back shortly." I then went back to the cabin and briefed our passengers who were obviously very disappointed with this unexpected turn of events. They understood the fear that SARS was causing around the world and seemed resigned to the fact that their well planned and anticipated Cyprus vacation was no more. To my co-Captain I said, "We are going to Madrid. We won't be able to get the Operational Flight Plan (OFP) faxed to us so I am going to call UV and ask for the flight plan number (with that number we can request and download it from the satellite via the aircraft's Flight Management System), cruise Mach number, Flight Level, and fuel required." This last bit of information, the realization that we would not get a hard copy of the OFP, caused him some consternation but he understood we were facing a highly irregular situation and needed to cope as best we could.

Flying a trip without a hard copy of the OFP was highly unusual and very uncomfortable but, as we proved later that day, it can be done safely. Once we were airborne I called UV again via the satellite phone and they provided all the additional information we needed from the OFP. With this information we were able to confirm our progress (i.e., time and fuel remaining) in relation to each waypoint along the route of flight. We had departed Larnaca with far more fuel than was required so we knew we would land with ample fuel reserves. While on our way to the Madrid-Barajas airport UV organized ground handling services, ground transportation, and hotel accommodations. Five hours and twenty minutes later we landed in Madrid, tired, but relieved that this ordeal was finally over. My crew and I had been presented with an extraordinary challenge but, together, we pulled it off, safely and effectively.

The rapid spread of the SARS epidemic was causing panic around the world and the Cypriot authorities simply reacted accordingly. It's just unfortunate that their decision to revoke our landing and parking permits was made while we were airborne and well on our way to Larnaca. As a result of this knee-jerk reaction we were placed in a very difficult situation. We couldn't just proceed to our flight plan's alternate airport because it too was located in Cyprus. We did not have sufficient fuel to simply turn around and return to Dubai. The closest countries to us were Syria, Lebanon, Jordan, Turkey, Saudi Arabia, Iraq, and Israel. That was a really bad neighborhood to suddenly find yourself in with limited fuel remaining in your tanks and without a landing permit. Had the Cypriot authorities refused to let us enter their airspace and land in Larnaca we would have had to declare a "Mayday, Mayday, Mayday" in order to land. When you declare a "Mayday" the air traffic controller is obligated to give your aircraft priority over every other aircraft and to render any and all assistance requested by the flight crew. The Captain has the ultimate authority, and final responsibility, to do whatever he deems necessary, including deviating from any rule, regulation or procedure, so as to ensure the safety of his passengers, crew, and aircraft. Fortunately we did not have to declare an emergency but, had they denied authorization to land, we had been fully prepared to do so. With limited remaining fuel onboard we were not going to take any chances.

Once we arrived in Cascais we notified the Civil Aviation Authority of Macao about the incident and asked them to raise this matter with the relevant government officials. We knew there was very little anyone could do to assuage the fear associated with SARS around the world. Nonetheless we felt that the decision to revoke our landing permit while we were in-flight, with very few options available, compromised our safety and deserved some scrutiny. As far as I know nothing ever came out of that report.

Fortunately the concerted effort by countries around the world to contain and eradicate SARS eventually produced results and, by January 2004, the epidemic ceased to exist. No new cases of SARS have developed since then but it is just a matter of time before another epidemic arises somewhere in the world. It's been many years since those days but whenever I think of SARS my thoughts always take me back to that dreadful day flying to Larnaca.

35

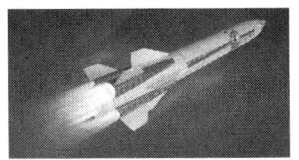

"Did he just say what I think he said?"

THE KEY TO THE SUCCESSFUL completion of any flight, whether a short-distance domestic flight or a long-distance international flight, is meticulous planning, timely preparation, precise execution, and the crew's ability to anticipate and cope with sudden changes. Every trip is unique. Some are more challenging than others and you can always count on last minute changes and surprises. For the most part, however, trips tend to be uneventful but never routine. Upon a successfully completed trip we derive a great sense of satisfaction knowing that we completed it safely, effectively, and efficiently. Every once in a while something happens, before or after departure, that makes an otherwise uneventful trip…unforgettable. What follows is the story of a meticulously planned and impeccably executed trip with an unexpected and bizarre twist. It happened on a flight from Paris to Hong

Kong in a Global Express, an ultra-long-range aircraft.

Long-range operations are challenging and very demanding because the aircraft is operated at its maximum weight limits and performance capabilities while flying over multiple countries and crossing numerous time zones. The bulk of the work, however, commences well before departure. A suitable aircraft is selected and prepared, a licensed and qualified flight and cabin crew is assigned and notified, overflight permits and landing slot(s) are requested and secured, ground handling services are requested and confirmed, customs, immigration, and quarantine requirements (CIQ) are determined and complied with, fuel purchase order is placed and approved, flight plan is duly prepared and timely submitted, airport runway analysis is requested and prepared, etc.

I personally like to begin preparing for these trips as many days in advance as possible. First, seven to ten days before departure I ask our dispatch office to provide daily flight plan packages consisting of an Operational Flight Plan (OFP), relevant Notices to Airmen (NOTAMs) and weather package. The OFP is a computer-generated document which shows, among many other things, the route of flight, flight levels, fuel requirements, cruising speeds, time enroute, average wind component, etc. The list of NOTAMs can be quite extensive but are important because they provide useful information about issues that could potentially affect the flight such as runway closures, instrument approach procedures and navigation aids out of service, airspace/airway restrictions, etc. The weather package includes winds/temperature charts for various levels, high level significant weather charts for the entire region, and the destination and alternate airports' reported (METAR) and forecast (TAF) weather reports. With regards to the weather package the idea is to start analyzing data to form a mental picture of what is happening. This is critical because it prepares you for what to expect. Second, I begin tracking the status of overflight permits and landing slot, ground handling services arrangements, CIQ notification, ground transportation requirements, crew hotel reservations, etc. Third, I ensure that the aircraft is airworthy, impeccably clean, and ready for departure from a regulatory and safety point of view. Fourth, because most intercontinental trips tend to be scheduled for departure close to midnight, my crew and I start preparing physically so as to be as well-rested as possible before departure. Somewhere in between all of these activities the Flight Attendant is busy assessing passengers' specific meal requirements, placing the corresponding catering order, and restocking the aircraft.

On this particular day we received the flight plan package via fax at the hotel four hours before the scheduled departure time. The OFP called for an estimated time enroute (ETE) of 11:55 hours, a cruise speed of Mach 0.83 (this is an optimum long-range speed for this aircraft), an average tailwind component of 35 knots, an initial cruise level of FL410 (41,000 feet) with a step climb to FL450 (45,000 feet), and a total fuel load of 42,200 pounds at brakes release. Based on these numbers we expected to land in Hong Kong with a reasonable 4,500 pounds of fuel reserve. That would be enough for us to execute an instrument approach into Hong Kong, carry out a missed approach procedure, enter a holding pattern for 30 minutes, divert to our alternate airport, and still have about 45 minutes of fuel remaining after landing. Weather enroute, as well as for our destination and alternate airports, was forecasted to be quite good.

We arrived at the airport two hours before departure, carried out a detailed briefing and a complete review of all trip documents. With pre-flight inspection duties (flight compartment checks and external walk around inspection) allocated we started getting the aircraft ready. Shortly after the fuel truck arrived we confirmed that it had the proper type of fuel (Jet A1), carried out a fuel contamination test, ensured the aircraft and fuel truck were properly grounded, and tested the aircraft fuel system (high level float/high pressure switches). Only then did we allow the fueling to start. The OFP called for 42,200 pounds of fuel so I wanted to see that much...or more. There are several techniques for attempting to pump more fuel into the tanks. For the Global Express these include parking the aircraft on level ground with a slightly nose down attitude, reducing the pressure of the fuel to 40 pounds per square inch (psi) as it enters the tanks in order to avoid foaming, using "Manual" versus "Automatic" refueling, transferring 200 to 300 pounds of fuel via gravity from the tail tank into the auxiliary tank when this one is full, then topping off the tail tank again, etc. How effective these "techniques" are is debatable. What isn't debatable is that fuel density determines how much fuel you can really count on. The colder the fuel is the more dense it is. The more dense the fuel is the heavier it is. This is critical because when it comes to aircraft range, fuel weight, not volume, is the determining factor. The Global Express fuel tanks can hold 43,550 pounds (at a specific fuel density and temperature) but in certain places, like Hong Kong, due to the effects of prevailing low fuel density the most I have seen is 41,000 pounds. On this particular trip we were departing from Paris' Le Bourget airport and, due to excellent fuel density, by the time the fuel truck finished refueling the fuel tank gauges showed an impressive 43,700 pounds. I was a very happy camper as this was about 1,500 pounds more than what was required by the flight plan. However, with the Auxiliary Power Unit (APU) powering all onboard electrical systems and supplying pneumatic bleed air for air conditioning, we would burn about 200 to 400 pounds of that fuel while waiting for our lone passenger. I asked the fuel truck driver to keep the fuel truck connected to the aircraft until our passenger arrived. He was happy to do so and, as our passenger boarded, we finished fueling. By the time I closed the main cabin door and settled in my seat the fuel gauges were showing 43,700 pounds of fuel again. It was a great feeling.

Air traffic control clearance was requested and promptly received. Shortly thereafter we received clearance to taxi to runway 09 for departure. There were no delays for departure and we were airborne within minutes heading eastbound over the French countryside. Passing through 10,000 feet we accelerated to 300 knots and maintained that speed until we transitioned to Mach 0.80. At our initial cruise altitude of FL410 we accelerated to Mach 0.83, completed the Cruise checklist, and began recording data on the OFP. Total fuel, as we lined up with the runway for takeoff, was a cool 43,400 pounds. We had burnt a meager 300 pounds during engine start and taxi to the runway. As a result we began the trip with an extra 1,200 pounds. Everything was progressing well as we flew across France into Germany, Poland, Russia, Ukraine, and Kazakhstan. As we burned fuel and the aircraft became lighter our fuel consumption per hour decreased. Eventually we were light enough to climb to FL450 which reduced our hourly fuel consumption even more. So far we were ahead on fuel and time over each waypoint along the airway. By the time we entered Chinese airspace and checked in with the controller we had transitioned to a cruising altitude of 13,700 meters (44,900 feet), had been in the air for about seven hours, and were doing better than the flight plan. I was very pleased with our progress. Unlike most countries around the world, China uses altitudes in meters instead of feet. The three onboard navigation computers were estimating 5,500 pounds of fuel remaining on arrival and this figure was confirmed by our own calculations. "Looking good so far," I quietly said to myself. That all changed when I returned from the lavatory and saw my co-Captain dialing down the altitude selector.

I quickly sat and strapped down, put on the headphones, and anxiously asked, "What's going on?" Sensing the concern in my voice my co-Captain answered, almost apologetically, "The controller just instructed us to descend to 10,100 meters." The first thing that went through my head was why would he want us to descend from 13,700 to 10,100 meters. As it did not make any sense, and concerned about the impact it would have on fuel, I said, "Don't descend. I have the radios."

With a sense of urgency I keyed the microphone and said, "Urumqi Control, November Six Niner Eight Mike Tango (N698MT), unable to accept 10,100 meters. Request climb." The controller's response came quickly, "N698MT, descend 10,100 meters." My response was just as quick, "Negative, N698MT unable to accept 10,100 meters. Destination Hong Kong." I was trying to get him to understand that a descent to 10,100 meters would adversely affect our ability to reach our destination due to higher fuel consumption at that lower altitude. After a brief pause he responded, "N698MT, descend 10,100 meters." My message clearly did not register so I decided to up the ante. "Unable to accept that clearance due to fuel. Repeat, fuel. Our destination is Hong Kong. If we descend we will be forced to land in Kunming." (Kunming is a Chinese city located approximately 643 nautical miles west of Hong Kong). There was a long pause and I wondered whether the controller understood what I was trying so hard to say. A different controller with a much better accent, and whom I suspected was the supervisor, came on the radio and said, "N698MT, Urumqi Control, you need to descend to 10,100 meters." To which I responded "Urumqi Control, N698MT, if we descend to 10,100 meters we will not be able to reach our destination and may need to land in Kunming. We want to maintain this level or climb to a higher level. Why do we have to descend?" What he said next blew us away, literally. "N698MT, we launch rocket." Almost immediately my co-Captain and I looked at each other and after a brief pause I asked, "Did he just say what I think he said? Is he threatening with shooting us down?" He nodded nervously and before he could say anything I keyed the microphone and asked, "Urumqi Control, N698MT, say again?" The controller probably sensed the concern in my voice and promptly said, "We launch rocket...to space." Ok, we were not being threatened with being shot down...and that was definitely good news, but I still did not want to descend, so I said, "Understand. We can accept radar vectors (a change of heading) but wish to maintain current flight level." There was a brief pause before he said, "N698MT, if you descend now to 10,100 meters you can climb again in 300 miles." At our current ground speed we could cover that distance in 35 minutes. Descending to such a low altitude was highly undesirable but, provided we did get a clearance to climb again in 35 minutes or so, I was willing to consider it. So I said, "Confirm that if we descend to 10,100 meters now we will be able to climb again to 13,700 meters in 300 miles, correct?" "Affirmative," he said. Given his assurances I responded, "N698MT descending 10,100 meters."

As we leveled off at 10,100 meters, despite an intentional reduction in our cruise speed to Mach 0.80, we observed with concern that our fuel consumption had increased considerably. The navigation computers predicted that, if we maintained that level until it was time to descend for landing, we would have 2,500 pounds of fuel remaining. To compound our situation even more we were experiencing some turbulence. So there we were: slowing down, burning more fuel, bouncing around, and with nearly five hours still remaining to go. I just couldn't see how descending from our flight plan cruise altitude of 13,700 meters to 10,100 meters, a difference of only 3,600 meters (11,800 feet), could make any difference on a rocket launch that was probably taking place hundreds of miles away from us. Just as frustrating, the NOTAMs we had reviewed before departure had not alerted us to any restrictions along our route of flight.

The air traffic controller kept his word and when we reached the agreed upon position he cleared us to climb to 13,700 meters. To compensate for the fuel we had lost at the lower altitude we maintained a cruise speed of Mach 0.80. The navigation computers now predicted that we would have 4,100 pounds of fuel on arrival. This quantity, while well below our initial estimates, still met regulatory fuel reserve requirements. Fortunately weather in Hong Kong was good so extensive delays were unlikely. By the time we finally touched down on Hong Kong's runway 07R the fuel gauges indicated a total of 3,800 pounds of fuel remaining. We were still legal and reasonably safe but only because we had been able to upload an extra 1,500 pounds of fuel in Paris' Le Bourget airport. Had fuel density been low…it would have been a completely different story.

I have flown around the world many times and thought I had already seen and heard it all. That bizarre exchange with the Chinese air traffic controller, and the momentary belief that we were about to be shot down for repeatedly refusing to comply with that controller's rigid and unreasonable instructions, certainly made this challenging trip different from all the others. It's not uncommon for air traffic control to assign lower flight levels in order to separate traffic…but never by that much. To my co-Captain, a very experienced contract pilot (short term contracts) I had recently hired and met, I respectfully offered a word of advice: "Don't accept an air traffic control clearance that will hurt you." The point being that by blindly accepting the air traffic controller's instructions you solve his problem and create one for yourself. To his credit he graciously, and wholeheartedly, accepted that advice. This had certainly been a challenging and exhausting trip, and there is no doubt that we both gained more experience that day. Years later we crossed paths again and had a "remember that time...?" moment. We both had a good chuckle. After all it isn't everyday that a couple of corporate pilots become entangled, and somehow interfere, with China's space program during the launch of one of its manned space flights.

The 19-story tall "Shenzhou-6" spacecraft was launched October 12, 2005 at 0900 A.M. from the Jiuquan Satellite Launch Center, Gansu Province, in northwest China. The spacecraft was carrying two astronauts, Fei Julong and Nie Haisheng, and reached orbit within minutes. Somewhere down below and hundreds of miles away a Chinese air traffic controller keyed his microphone and said, "N698MT, climb 13,700 meters."

36

"Your name Ivan?"

HAVING DONE MY SHARE OF traveling over the previous three decades I have seen and done many things. Every once in a while I come across what I consider to be a memorable experience...even if at the time I did not see it that way. What follows is one such event. It happened at the Petropavlovsk airport.

Petropavlovsk is a Russian city located in a rather isolated peninsula and due to its geographical location, the North Pacific, its winters are long and very cold. Its airport served as a Soviet military base during the cold war. With the collapse of the Soviet Union, and the Russian economy in shambles, the government decided to allow foreign civilian aircraft to use the airport as a fuel stop and transit point between North America and Asia. In exchange they collected desperately needed foreign currency. As a result I have landed at the Petropavlovsk airport on numerous occasions over the years. I have found it to be ideally located within the range capabilities of most small to medium size business aircraft whether departing eastbound from Tokyo, Japan, or westbound from Anchorage, Alaska.

On arrival, crews are met by a local ground handling agent who then escorts the Captain to the main airport terminal in order to clear immigration and complete other arrival/departure formalities while the other pilot stays with the aircraft overseeing the refueling process and getting it ready for departure. Then, upon the Captain's return, the other pilot is escorted to the terminal to clear immigration. One thing I noted, from body language and tone of voice, was that the immigration officer who handled the passports always seemed unfriendly. That is not to say that all immigration officers at the Petropavlovsk airport or at any other Russian airports are unfriendly. For some reason I just happened to always come across an unfriendly one during my stopovers. Immigration officers have a crucial and difficult job. On the one hand they serve as Ambassadors representing their respective countries – they are typically the first contact an arriving visitor has with someone from that country. On the other hand they also serve as law enforcement officers. In this capacity they are last line of defense when foreigner visitors arrive in their country – a task which confirms visitors meet established entry requirements and can be allowed in or that criminals are not permitted to enter and stay in the country. As a world traveler I have seen my share of immigration officers. What follows is an unusual, and somewhat terse, exchange with one such officer at the Petropavlovsk airport.

In 2007 I found myself ferrying four mid-range aircraft from the U.S. to Macao. Due to duty time limitations an overnight in Anchorage was planned for the first day. The following day we would land in Petropavlovsk to refuel and then continue on to Osaka, Japan, for another overnight. On the last day we would land in Taipei, Taiwan, for fuel and then continue to Macao. I flew these ferry flights with four different, and recently hired, pilots who I was training. While enroute to Petropavlovsk I would share with them details about the time one of my First Officers and I overnighted in this Russian city just to see what it would be like. That story about eating fish and potatoes for dinner...and potatoes and fish for breakfast served by the same no-nonsense woman who took pity on us always made everyone laugh.

When I handed my passport to the immigration officer she took a look at it and with a strong Russian accent, drily asked me, "Your name Ivan?" "Yes," I answered. Without looking at me she then asked, "You have Russian name?" "Yes," I answered. Then, in her most unfriendly tone and heavily accented voice, she looked at me and asked me point blank, "Why?" I was completely taken aback by the question and her bluntness but I answered by saying that I was named after my father and that his own father had named him Ivan because he had been a communist sympathizer in the 1930s. She seemed somewhat pleased with this last bit of information. Then she asked, "Your last name Luciani?" "Yes," I answered. To which she replied in an almost accusatory tone, "You have Russian name *and* Italian last name?" "Yes," I answered with some trepidation. Then, still feeling very uncomfortable with her open animosity, I said, "That means that I like to drink my vodka when I eat pizza." Suddenly, the most remarkable and unexpected thing happened. For the first time in the entire conversation she gave me a broad smile, and what a beautiful smile it was. Then, with that beautiful smile completely vanished and without uttering another word or even looking at me, she promptly stamped and handed back my passport. I then turned around and was then escorted back to the ramp so that I could stay at the aircraft while my co-Captain cleared immigration. As I walked back to the aircraft I asked myself, "vodka *and* pizza, seriously? How in the world did I come up with that?"

I don't really drink vodka when eating pizza but when I either drink vodka (hardly ever) or eat pizza (often) doing so always takes me back to that day in Petropavlovsk. Nasdrovie (cheers), Russia!

37

Goodbye, Macao!

PERHAPS THE MOST IMPORTANT CHAPTER in my professional career was the eleven years I invested on Jet ExecuAir. Not so much because of the length of time, which in itself is significant, but because of the opportunity to put into practice everything I knew as a manager. There were certainly many ups and downs but I loved this company and considered it an important part of me.

The company was founded in 1997 and shortly thereafter was issued an Air Operator's Certificate (AOC) by the Civil Aviation Authority of Macao (also spelled Macau). Its Chairman had been actively involved in Macao's development for many years. Its first aircraft, a Challenger 601-3R, was purchased in 1995 and operated initially by its sister company, a helicopter airline that provided scheduled international passenger service between three cities in the region. Having been involved in the construction of the airport and the establishment of a local airline, the Chairman decided to purchase an executive business jet and base it permanently at the newly built airport. Bombardier Aerospace was the only aircraft manufacturer able to commit to the sale and on-time delivery of one of its business jets in time for the opening of the airport. Hence the decision to purchase a brand new Challenger 601-3R was made.

Macao would remain a Portuguese colony until December 20, 1999, when the official handover to China took place. After over 400 years as a Portuguese-administered territory and colony this was a historical event and we were there to witness it. After the handover Macao became known as Macao Special Administrative Region (MSAR) of the People's Republic of China. Under China's "one country, two systems," this old colony would be permitted to preserve its Portuguese-based legal system for a period of 50 years. This was a significant concession that included, among other things, aviation regulations and standards closely aligned with Europe's.

I joined Jet ExecuAir on August 1, 1999, as a Challenger Captain and left on August 22, 2010, as its Director of Flight Operations. During my first few weeks with the company several things became evident. It was a close-knit operation, almost like a family. It was well-funded and money wasn't an issue. It seemed like a great place to work. However, it lacked well thought-out and documented policies, procedures, and processes. Its Aviation Manager, Roger Lewis, wanted to grow the company and believed I could help him. Roger had been eager to hire me and as soon as I joined the company he asked me to become the Chief Pilot. Realizing that he was a micromanager who wanted to be involved in every decision, regardless of how small, I was reluctant to accept. I knew, and was concerned, that it would put us on a collision course. His frequent assurances however, to provide me the space, resources, and support to do whatever I considered necessary to help him take Jet ExecuAir to the next level, persuaded me, a couple of months later, to accept the Chief Pilot position.

When, several months earlier, I was first invited to visit Jet ExecuAir I had dinner with David, its most senior Captain. I told him that I was impressed with everything I had seen but wanted his personal assessment of what it was like to work with Roger. He assured me that working with him was great, that I would enjoy doing so, and he encouraged me to accept the job. Fast-forward to September, a month after I joined the company. I asked him, "David, do you remember when we had dinner a few months ago and I asked you about Roger?" "Yes," he said. "Why didn't you tell me how he really was?" I asked frustratedly. "Ivan, would you have accepted the job if I had told you how he was?" he asked. "No way," I said. "That's why I never told you! He wanted to hire you so badly that I wasn't going to say, or do, anything to screw up his plans," he stated. Roger may have had difficulty delegating but he was also the kind of guy who would stick his neck out, and put his own job on the line, for his staff. You couldn't ask for a better friend either. He was the kind of person we could always count on. The one trait I admire and respect the most about him was his sense of integrity. I also have to give him credit for hiring me. Not only did he believe I had the experience and qualifications necessary to help him but he knew I was also a workaholic who, like him, would produce results. I am, and will always remain, grateful to him for hiring me and believing in me.

Over the following years the company grew exponentially but for me it all began with a blank piece of paper, a pen, and a little bit of observation on my part. The company lacked written procedures and processes even though there were a number of things that were done consistently and in a standardized manner. Our first two priorities were: a) to identify what it was that the company did, how it did it, and to document it and b) to develop and maintain a relationship with the Civil Aviation Authority of Macao based on mutual respect and trust. I was a manager while concurrently performing line pilot duties. In this dual and challenging capacity being one made me better at the other. Spending time in the trenches with the pilot group gave me the opportunity to see first-hand what worked, what did not and, most importantly, what needed to be done in order to make it work. As a manager I was then in an excellent position to implement whatever changes were required. One of the most important lessons I learned, and one I fully embraced, was that an effective manager was someone who recognized and appreciated the fact that it took well-trained and highly motivated individuals to accomplish the company's mission. To that effect we implemented the following three-phase process: a) attract and hire individuals with the right attitude, personality, qualifications, and experience b) retain these individuals by giving them the best training possible, provide them the support to make good decisions, give them the tools they need to do their jobs and, just as importantly, treat and pay them well and c) convert them into stakeholders who would invest themselves, and take on an ownership role in the well-being of the company. The outcome of this three-phase process was a highly devoted, loyal, and capable workforce that moved in unison towards a common goal and took pride in what they did and how they did it. These individuals were fully prepared to go the extra mile for the company and did so each and every time. In essence THEY became the Company and made it what it was – a great company. I consider myself honored to have worked with such remarkable professionals.

One of the most important tasks we accomplished early-on was writing the Flight Operations Manual (FOM). This comprehensive manual, reviewed and revised several times over the years, clearly defined what it was that we did and how we did it. It accurately represented who we were as a company and what our mission was. In essence it became our bible and a source of great pride for each one of us. To give it the full weight that it represented I asked our Chairman to sign the cover page under the following statement, "The Flight Operations Manual is an official Company document and has been reviewed and approved by the Board of Directors and Executive Management. It provides detailed procedures and guidelines for the safe operation of the Company's aircraft. All items contained in this document must be followed with the highest level of professionalism and standardization. When Flight Operations personnel act in accordance with these procedures they do so with the full support of the Board of Directors and Executive Management." This statement, and the Chairman's signature below it, became a contract between the users of the manual and the Chairman. No one, not even the Chairman, could ever ask us to deviate from the high standards that this manual represented.

In May 2006, our company was selected to be profiled in *Professional Pilot* magazine. This monthly magazine is well known among professional pilots as a source of aviation-related news and information. The profile included the magazine's cover as well as the feature article that gave a detailed description of the company's flight and maintenance operations. This was a significant recognition to the professionalism that we represented as a company and we were incredibly proud of this achievement.

In mid 2007 a decision to lease and operate a fleet of six small sized business jets resulted in the gradual dismantling of this great company. From an operational, maintenance, and regulatory point of view we accomplished everything that was required to incorporate and operate these small business jets. Unfortunately, the business plan proved to be flawed and these business jets were simply the wrong type of aircraft for the region and clientele. As a result this massive project never got off the ground and eventually had to be abandoned. That fleet of business jets has since gone, but the effects of that decision are still being felt today within the company. There is, however, something positive that came out of this failed project and which I cherish very much: my relationship with Eddy Vercelli. I had known and worked with Eddy in Singapore several years earlier so I hired him as the Chief Pilot and put him in charge of the Hawker fleet and its crews. He was instrumental in developing and implementing the procedures, processes, and policies necessary to operate these aircraft under the provisions of our AOC. Our working relationship soon developed into a friendship built on trust, loyalty, mutual respect, and genuine concern for each other. As a proud U.S. Marine and Vietnam veteran, Eddy's sense of honor, loyalty, and integrity are unparalleled. I proudly consider him my big brother. In addition to my parents this book is also dedicated to him. Semper Fi, Eddy.

One of the joys of working for this company was the opportunity to get to know the Chairman well. Always a gentleman, he was a caring and reasonable person who extended his unconditional support to me on more than one occasion. Early on during my first few weeks in the company and after I had flown with him for the first time on a challenging 10-day trip to Europe, we would get a call from the Chairman's office requesting a trip that quoted him as saying, "I want the pilot with the Italian last name." Within a few months I was no longer the pilot with the Italian last name but simply "Ivan." One of the books in my personal library that I treasure the most is a biography of the Chairman that he dedicated, signed, and gave to me. My colleagues and I will always have a great deal of respect, appreciation, and loyalty for him.

As it eventually happens I reached a point in which I was ready for a change. I admit that it was a difficult decision leaving a company to which I had devoted so many years of my life but I am absolutely convinced that it was the right decision. Those eleven years were the longest I had ever worked for a company and, during that time, I gave it absolutely everything I had. By the time I left, the company had a well-established system with the necessary foundations in place to support its mission. That mission was to provide our Chairman, his family and friends, as well as to our distinguished charter clients, safe and efficient air transportation. We had a credible safety culture and program, a well known reputation in the region, and enjoyed a nearly zero turnover rate. Thanks to the high degree of professionalism and capacity displayed by my colleagues there was never an accident, incident, or safety violation. Furthermore, the level of trust with the Civil Aviation Authority of Macao was the highest it had ever been. Those of us who worked for this great company can look back with a great sense of pride at the many lasting and tangible contributions we accomplished together. The day I left an important chapter in my personal and professional career closed, but another one was about to open. There was only one other company I wanted and aspired to work for – a company with an impeccable reputation for excellence based in the bustling city of Hong Kong.

Before I left Macao, however, I offered my services as an unpaid consultant for a period of two years. I explained that I was making that offer as a sign of my appreciation, respect, and loyalty towards the Chairman as well as because of my love for the company. The offer was gladly accepted. Over the following two years, I provided advice through a member of the Board of Directors on a number of areas related to the operation of a company into which I had invested so many years of my life. When those two years as a consultant were over it was finally time for me to say goodbye…one last time.

Goodbye, Macao!

38

Hello, Hong Kong!

HONG KONG IS ONE OF the most modern, dynamic, and safest cities in the world. It is also one of the best places in Asia for expatriates to live and work because, among many other things, of its generous hospitality and cosmopolitan atmosphere. After the handover, July 1, 1997, this former British colony became officially known as the Hong Kong Special Administrative Region (HKSAR) of the People's Republic of China. Under China's "one country, two systems," Hong Kong had been permitted to preserve its English Common Law system for a period of 50 years. This arrangement included, among other things, aviation regulations and standards closely aligned with Europe's.

Hong Kong's old airport, Kai Tak, was well known among pilots because of its challenging approach to runway 13. This technically-demanding approach required the pilot to make a last minute, 47 degree visual right turn at low altitude over a densely populated area. This highly unusual maneuver, affectionately called the "Checkerboard turn" or "Hong Kong turn," was required in order for the pilot to line up the aircraft with the runway. The Instrument Guidance System (IGS) gave the pilot electronic lateral and vertical guidance down to a point in which he had to be in visual contact with a large white and orange checkerboard on the side of a hill. The challenge for the pilot was then to correctly judge the effect of the wind as he made the turn so as not to overshoot or touch down at awkward angle. I had the opportunity to fly to Kai Tak on a few occasions and can certainly attest to its reputation. To execute this approach after a long intercontinental trip, and during nighttime marginal weather conditions, is quite difficult for the pilot. This is particularly so when you consider the cumulative effect of fatigue and its effect on performance. One day I had the chance to see what that maneuver looked like from the window of my hotel. We had just checked in and I was in my room when I decided to look out the window. I opened the curtains and gasped when I saw a Boeing 747 that appeared to be coming straight at me…and it kept getting bigger and bigger! Suddenly it started to turn as the pilot skillfully lined up the enormous aircraft with the runway. That was quite a sight. There were a few cases over the years where pilots misjudged the turn and touched down too far down the runway. Without enough runway remaining to stop the aircraft, their aircraft ended up in the water. Parking space for aircraft was limited so we were often required to drop off our passengers and then fly the short hop to neighboring Macao for overnight parking. The day of departure we would then fly back to Kai Tak, execute the dreaded approach and land, pick up our passengers, and depart for our next destination. Flying in and out of Kai Tak was an amazing experience and I was happy to have had the opportunity to do so. Having said that, I was absolutely delighted when the new airport opened up. Something tells me I wasn't the only pilot who felt that way.

A city as vibrant as Hong Kong desperately needed a new airport in order to cope with existing demand and projected growth. Enter Chek Lap Kok airport, which opened July 6, 1998. This is one of the most modern airports in the world. It is entirely built on reclaimed land on what is, in essence, an artificial island. It has two 12,000-foot runways equipped with an Instrument Landing System (ILS) on all four ends. I vividly remember my first trip to this remarkable airport. We had just landed on runway 07R and, after vacating the runway, received instructions to taxi to the brand new Business Aviation Center (BAC). When we got there we noted a huge ramp, hardly any other business jets, a large hangar, and an office/terminal building. Both were under construction. There was also a trailer-type office like the ones you see on large construction sites that served as the temporary terminal building. We must have been among the first visitors because its manager, a very friendly guy who had worked for many years for one of the largest Fixed Based Operator (FBO) chains in the U.S. (private aircraft terminals), came over to welcome us and to proudly tell us about this new facility. It was quite a sight and I wish I had taken pictures.

Fast-forward to 2015. The BAC now has three large hangars, a modern two-story tall office and passenger terminal, and its large ramp is often crowded with all types of business jets – mostly large cabin, ultra-long range aircraft. Growth over the previous 10 years has been such that the huge empty ramp we saw that day many years ago is now insufficient to handle the large number of resident and visiting aircraft. In fact, it's not uncommon for inbound passengers to be dropped off and for the aircraft to then fly to another airport for overnight parking, just like in the old days at Kai Tak. Despite the dramatic increase in business jet activity in Hong Kong the BAC continues to be recognized by pilots as being among the best private jet terminals in Asia. I can certainly attest to that assessment. We would love to see a few more facilities like the BAC around Asia.

Having reached a decision to seek a change after eleven years working for my previous employer in Macao I knew there was one specific company I wanted to work for. I had been following its progress since 1999 and was impressed with its long history, impeccable reputation, professional flight operations, and commitment to excellence. None of the other aircraft management companies in Hong Kong or the entire region came close to it. As of this writing it's been five years since I joined this great company.

It is hard to predict what the future holds in store for me. My hope, and intention, is to continue being a part of this company for the eleven years I have left before I turn 65 years old. That is when I plan to hang up my wings and retire. I readily invested eleven years of my life and career at my previous company and I will gladly invest my remaining years with my current employer. I would consider being able to do this as an amazing way to conclude this wonderful journey. There are, however, numerous factors in this line of business that are just beyond my control. Events like SARS, the 1998 Asian financial crisis, the 2007 stock market collapse and other such events can adversely affect business aviation. As aviators we understand and accept that this is the reality and nature of our line of work. Therefore, only time will tell whether this will be the last company I ever work for. For now this particular chapter of my professional career will have to remain unfinished.

I love Hong Kong!

39

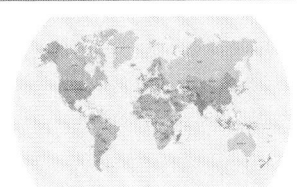

"Ivan, you've ruined the competition!"

A FEW YEARS AGO A good friend and colleague of mine shared with me a story about a competition he was currently involved in with a good friend of his. The competition, unofficially known as "I'll kick your arse at the most countries visited," had been going on for many years and, as the name implies, consisted of counting and comparing how many countries they had each visited. Their rules stated that, if a passport was required for entry, it counted as a "country." Whoever had been to the most countries earned bragging rights over the loser. At the time my co-Captain had visited 39 countries and was winning the competition by a large margin. Then he casually asked, "Ivan, how many countries have you visited?" I had never actually counted, or even cared to know, how many countries I had been to. I knew that it was a lot of them, but I couldn't think of even an approximate number so

I simply said, "I think I have been to about 30 countries."

For a couple of weeks after the above conversation I had all but forgotten about it but for some reason the question suddenly popped into my head. Although I had no desire to participate in their competition I felt a sudden curiosity to know how many countries I had actually visited. That's how I decided to take a piece of paper and a pen and start writing the names of every country and territory I could remember having visited. It took me a while to come up with what I thought was an accurate list which I then organized by continent and region. I showed the list to my lovely wife who, with her sharp memory, reminded me of a few countries that I had forgotten to include. By the time I was certain that the list was complete the total was 69 countries and 14 non-sovereign territories. I knew I had visited many countries and territories, both as a pilot and a tourist, but I must admit that even I was surprised by how many.

A couple of days later I brought the subject up with my colleague. I said, "You remember when you asked me how many countries I had visited and I said that it was about 30 countries?" "Yes," he answered. "Well, I was curious to actually know so I decided to write down on a piece of paper each country I have visited. I have now come up with the exact number of countries. Would you like to know how many?" "Sure," he said. To which I responded, "69 countries." I never mentioned to him that the total, as high as it already was, did not include territories. After a brief pause he said, "How can we ever compete with that number?" Then, half-jokingly and half-seriously, he stated, "Ivan, you've ruined the competition!" Here is the list:

NORTH AMERICA (3):
Canada, Mexico, and the United States of America.

CENTRAL AMERICA (6):
Costa Rica, El Salvador, Guatemala, Honduras, Nicaragua, and Panama.

SOUTH AMERICA (6):
Brazil, Colombia, Ecuador, Peru, Suriname, and Venezuela.

CARIBBEAN (3):
Cuba, the Dominican Republic, and Trinidad and Tobago.

EUROPE/MEDITERRANEAN (21):
Austria, Belgium, Cyprus, Czech Republic, Denmark, France, Germany, Greece, Italy, Ireland, Monaco, Montenegro, the Netherlands, Portugal, Russia, Spain, Switzerland, Turkey, the United Kingdom, Ukraine, and Vatican City.

MIDDLE EAST (4):
Bahrain, Kuwait, Qatar, and the United Arab Emirates (Dubai).

ASIA (24):
Bangladesh, Brunei, Cambodia, China, East Timor, India, Indonesia, Japan, Kazakhstan, Laos, Malaysia, the Maldives, Mongolia, Myanmar, Nepal, North Korea, Papua New Guinea, Pakistan, the Philippines, Singapore, South Korea, Sri Lanka, Thailand, and Vietnam.

SOUTH PACIFIC (2):
Australia and the Marshall Islands (Majuro).

Visited but not counted due to their non-sovereign status (14):
Aruba, American Samoa, Bonaire, Christmas Island, Curacao, Guam, Hong Kong, Macao, Midway, Puerto Rico, Saint Martin, Sint Maarten, Taiwan, and the U.S. Virgin Islands.

How many countries a professional pilot travels to during his or her career depends on many, many factors. In the course of a forty-year career an airline or corporate pilot could travel to as few as a dozen countries or as many as a hundred. Another friend of mine has visited 95 countries and territories so far and has a more impressive list than mine. It all depends on which companies you've worked for and the length of your career. In the case of an airline pilot it could be just a few countries or many of them depending on the airline he or she works for. But even working for a major international carrier the number of countries traveled to will also depend on the aircraft type assigned (e.g., an A319 on regional trips or a B777 on intercontinental trips). Airline destinations vary from time to time and are selected primarily on profitability expectations. Similarly, how many countries a corporate pilot travels to depends largely on whether the companies he or she worked for had domestic or international operations, or both. In addition, the aircraft types flown (e.g., a short-range Citation II or an ultra-long range Global Express) is a big factor also. For these companies the corporate aircraft is a tool that allows them to reach their customers wherever they are and that includes many destinations not always served by airlines. As a result, for a corporate pilot the list of countries visited can be quite extensive and varied.

As I reflect on the places that I have already traveled to there are a few additional countries that I would love to visit someday. Among these are New Zealand, Fiji, and Iceland – countries that I think are unique and exotic. There are many countries I have visited while on personal trips with my family which were selected based on previous experiences when I visited them as a pilot. Regardless of how large or small your personal list of countries visited is, being a professional pilot is a wonderful way to see the world…or, as an experienced pilot and good friend of mine countered, "…or just a bunch of airports." As I said earlier, it all depends.

By the way, my colleague recently added 5 more countries, including Iceland, to his already impressive list. What I find even more amazing is how he visited one of those five countries. It happened while he was in Milan, Italy, during a trip. Concluding that the Swiss border was less than an hour away he hopped in a taxi, drove across the Swiss border, arrived at a coffee shop, had a coffee with the taxi driver, and then returned to Milan. While he had been sipping his made-in-Switzerland latte he couldn't help but send a picture to his friend saying, "I just added Switzerland to the list!" He just cracks me up. I still don't want to join their competition but must admit that I absolutely love that story. Way to go my friend!

40

Global Express and Gulfstream 550 – two very different technological marvels

IT'S EVERY PILOT'S DREAM TO eventually have the opportunity to fly bigger, faster, longer range, and more advanced aircraft. Yes, ego and a bigger paycheck are parts of it, but perhaps even more importantly it's the desire to master a new challenge.

I have been fortunate enough to have had the rare privilege of sitting at the controls of the two most advanced and prestigious ultra-long range business jets in production: the Bombardier Global Express (GEX) and the Gulfstream 550 (G550). Although these two magnificent airplanes are designed with high speed and altitude, and ultra-long range missions in mind, their design philosophy and operation couldn't be more different. Pilots and maintenance engineers often ask me which aircraft I consider the better of the two. The answer to that question is not quite so straight-forward as they are both excellent aircraft with individual strengths and weaknesses.

The Global Express is a 6,000 nautical mile (nm) business jet built by Bombardier Aerospace, a Canadian company. The aircraft was designed from scratch as a fully automated, systems integrated, wide body, and ultra-long range aircraft. The ample cockpit incorporates the "black cockpit concept," where a quick glance of the panels confirms whether everything is OK with the various systems (switchlight black) or not OK (switchlight illuminated). The aircraft's Crew Alerting System (CAS) gives the pilot visual and aural warnings as well as loud verbal announcements, such as a male voice stating "Engine Fire!" There is a considerable amount of redundancy in its systems that provide for, and ensure, a desirable level of safety during Extended Range Operations (EROs). No matter what the system failure might be when you are 180 or 240 minutes away from a suitable airport you'll always have what you need to get safely on the ground. For example the electrical system, the brains of the aircraft, consists of four (4) engine-driven AC generators, an APU-driven AC generator, and a Ram Air Turbine (RAT) which drives yet another AC generator. A single AC generator is capable of powering most systems needed in flight. The hydraulic system consists of three separate and independent hydraulic sub-systems, each one powered by two hydraulic pumps. That's six hydraulic pumps, plus yet another RAT-driven hydraulic pump. That's a considerable amount of redundancy. The wings incorporate leading edge devices (slats) that allow takeoff and landing operations on short runways. The wide-body cabin is ample, quiet, and designed with passenger comfort in mind.

The Gulfstream 550 (G550) is a 6,750 nm business jet built by the Gulfstream Aerospace Corporation (GAC), a U.S. company. The aircraft evolved from previous generations of Gulfstream aircraft dating back to the original Gulfstream I turboprop design from the late 1950s. The G550 is an improved and more advanced and capable version of each aircraft it superseded. Pilots of previous Gulfstream models can make the transition to newer versions quite easily. Preserving what works, adding continued improvements, and keeping it simple plus excellent product support have been GAC's recipe for success. The G550 systems are not nearly as sophisticated, integrated or redundant as the GEX's, but perform consistently well. As a result the aircraft accomplishes its mission with a high level of reliability that has earned it tremendous loyalty among pilots, operators, and owners. In addition to remarkable aircraft reliability and performance, GAC's unwavering commitment to product support and customer service remains the industry's best. Their mission is to ensure that when something breaks you get the necessary support to have it fixed and back in the air with minimum disruption. The cabin, although not as wide as the GEX's, is quiet and comfortable. Gulfstream aircraft are rugged, can take a lot of abuse, and are designed to last. The cockpit is a mixture of new technology combined with the old. The Honeywell PlaneView avionics system is very advanced and yet most of the other cockpit systems require manual input from the pilot which adds to their workload. Pressing a switchlight IN does not mean the selected system is ON just as depressing another switchlight OUT does not mean the selected system is OFF. Some aircraft systems use degrees Fahrenheit and others Celsius, or both. Gulfstream pilots readily accept, and forgive, this lack of consistency and standardization because they absolutely love everything else about the aircraft.

The GEX's systems are far more advanced and sophisticated but that introduces reliability problems associated with complexity. Bombardier's product support and customer service have improved considerably over the years and are now closely behind GAC's. The GEX's interior is absolutely beautiful but I found the knobs and rails from doors, cabinets, and drawers to be quite delicate when compared to those used in the G550. The G550's systems are far less advanced and sophisticated and there is far less cockpit automation but that results in greater system reliability and aircraft dispatchability. Pilots transitioning to a newer Gulfstream model, like the new G650, can do so easily as they find the systems' design and operation familiar. GAC is ranked as the industry's leader in terms of product support and customer service. This remarkable recognition has earned it the loyalty of aircraft owners who say their next aircraft will always be another Gulfstream.

Both manufacturers understand that having excellent

product support translates into happy customers. A happy customer is likely to become a repeat customer. A repeat customer ensures more aircraft sales. More aircraft sales is the name of the game. Bombardier Aerospace already builds, what in my opinion is, a more technologically sophisticated aircraft. If their product support continues to improve, as it has over the last several years, there is no reason to doubt it could eventually surpass GAC as the industry's leader.

My longest trips in a GEX to date have been Honolulu to Hong Kong in 11 hours and 30 minutes, Hong Kong to San Francisco in 11 hours and 45 minutes, Paris to Hong Kong in 12 hours and 10 minutes, and Toronto to Tokyo in 12 hours and 15 minutes. My longest trips in a G550 have been Paris to Hong Kong in 11 hours and 45 minutes and Hong Kong to London in 12 hours and 44 minutes. These trips were flown at a cruise speed between Mach 0.80 and 0.83 (maximum speed Mach 0.88). Initial, intermediate, and final cruise levels were 41,000, 43,000, 45,000 and 47,000 feet (maximum service ceiling 51,000 feet). Both aircraft performed exceedingly well and were a complete joy to fly.

In conclusion, I really like the GEX's advanced cockpit automation, systems design philosophy, easy-to-follow abnormal/emergency checklist structure, the availability of autobrakes, and its spacious cockpit and cabin. The aircraft's biggest drawback, however, are a slightly lower level of dispatchability associated with its more sophisticated systems and slightly shorter range due to its bigger size and weight. As far as the G550 is concerned I am impressed with its high level of reliability, performance (i.e., climb capability and range), as well as GAC's superb product and customer support. The aircraft's biggest drawback, however, are a much lower level of system automation, lack of a black cockpit design, lack of standardization with systems' temperature indications (i.e., Fahrenheit and Celsius), lack of consistency with switchlight position (i.e., pressed in or pushed out) and corresponding indications (i.e., ON, OFF, FAIL or blank), difficult-to-follow abnormal/emergency checklist structure, and a much narrower cockpit and cabin. Regardless of these drawbacks, having had the opportunity to fly both of these impressive aircraft has truly been a great privilege indeed.

On a final note, as a Lead Captain currently flying a brand new G550 since 2012, I often hear from Global Express pilots who, half-jokingly and half-seriously, say that I have gone over to the "Dark side." They express hope, however, that someday I will return to their side and have the opportunity to fly the Rockwell Collins Vision Flight Deck-equipped Global 5000 or 6000 or even the next generation Global 7000. Feeling a little envious every time I see pictures of the new Global's advanced cockpit design I say to them, "Who knows, someday I might just return to the bright side." Regardless of which way it goes I feel I have a much better understanding of, and appreciation for, these two technological marvels than I would have had if I had not been so privileged to experience both sides.

41

"Who do you work for?"

ONE OF THE JOYS OF accumulating experience over the years is being in a position to offer sound advice to those younger pilots who are in desperate need of it. However, dispensing advice must be handled with care as not everyone, even those who need it the most, are open to it. Many years ago a senior pilot told me, "Ivan, you can lead a horse to water, but you cannot make it drink." I had never heard that expression before, but there was no question in my mind that even that analogy represented sound advice.

Experience comes through exposure, over the course of many years, to a variety of situations, conditions, and circumstances. This is particularly so in cases where an error, regardless of who commits it, results in a lesson being learned. It's important to then share that experience with others so that they can also benefit from it. Every once in a while I come across a junior pilot, and occasionally even a senior pilot, seeking some much needed advice. As these junior pilots embark in their careers the best advice I can offer is when I ask them, "Who do you work for?"

The answer I receive is predictable and quick. "I work for Pacific Jetways," or whichever company their employer happens to be. To which I say, "No, you don't." They look at me quizzically for a few seconds as if trying to figure out what is the point I am trying to make. After a brief moment they answer confidently, "I work for the Owner of the aircraft I am assigned to. After all, he pays my salary." To which I say, "No, you don't." By then they are absolutely puzzled and start to look at me with total confusion wondering what could possibly be the correct answer to what is, in their mind, a simple question. This is when I offer them what I think is the best advice they are likely to ever receive as junior pilots.

I say, "You work for the Joe Smith (I use their actual name) Corporation. In this Corporation you hold the posts of CEO, President, and Chairman of the Board of Directors. In addition, you are also a shareholder. Your wife and each one of your kids are also equal shareholders and members of the Board of Directors. Your job as CEO, President, and Chairman of the Board is to ensure the financial and emotional well-being of your shareholders and members of the Board. Every decision that you ever make and every action you ever take have to be with yours and that of your shareholders' well-being in mind. Don't ever forget that."

By then the expression on their faces tells me that not only do they get it but they agree wholeheartedly. Then I expand further by telling them that doing what's best for the members of their Board and shareholders means being the best at what they do. It means taking great pride in what they do and how they do it. It means being loyal, dedicated, and diligent. It means going the extra mile at work each and every day. It means doing far more than what they get paid to do. It means acting with integrity. It means working on their personal development by continuously learning, mastering, and applying new skills. Jim Rohn, a well known motivational speaker, said that "the essence of life is growth...to do the best that you possibly can." To a large degree that statement captures what I am trying to say because when you do the best that you possibly can, not only will you grow professionally and personally, your shareholders and the members of your Board will benefit also. The same motivational speaker said that "success is not something that you seek. Success is something you attract." Excellent advice. Doing the best that you possibly can attracts success...and success enhances the well-being of your shareholders and members of the Board. Similarly, doing the best that you possibly can also means being able to recognize and then pursue any internal or external opportunities that help advance your career to new heights. Sure, there are always risks when pursuing job opportunities elsewhere but if you have done your due diligence, and made the right choice at the right time, chances are that you will be glad you took the chance.

I have been fortunate to have had the opportunity, and the rare privilege, to have always worked for great companies. As can be expected, even at these great companies, there were ups and there were downs. However, for the most part these companies provided me, and my colleagues, a working environment that fostered in us a desire to go the extra mile. I often sought, and was given, the opportunity to contribute and share my knowledge and experience with others. Furthermore, I also welcomed the opportunity to learn from others...even if that sometimes meant learning what not to do or, as a very experienced Gulfstream pilot said, "I learned from the worst." During my employment in each one of these companies I was loyal and diligent. I strived to make meaningful and lasting contributions and feel that, in some small tangible way, I left them in better shape than they were when I joined them. I honored my commitments and obligations, consistently represented them as best I could, and ensured that their good standing was always enhanced.

I also consider myself quite fortunate to have been offered many jobs over the years. Some of these offers came from people who only knew me by reputation. If a particular job offer did not contribute in a significant way towards enhancing the well-being of my shareholders and members of the Board, meaning better stability, salary and benefits, as well as the opportunity for future growth, I turned it down. In these cases however, I was careful to always decline in as professional a manner as possible while, at the same time, attempting to find and recommend someone else who was equally, if not more so, qualified than I was. Every one of the efforts described earlier has greatly enhanced my qualifications and reputation, and just as importantly, they have given me the opportunity for continued growth. In other words, they all helped open doors for me.

The bottom line is that as CEO, President, and Chairman of the Ivan Luciani Corporation an important part of my job has been to enhance my personal and professional qualifications as well as to recognize when the right opportunity for further advancement comes along. After all, the shareholders and members of my Board depend, expect, and have consistently counted on me to always remember the correct answer to "Who do you work for?" In the process of constantly striving to do the best that I possibly can I have been able to provide my loving, happy, and caring family the financial stability and emotional well-being they deserve. It just doesn't get any better than that, does it?

Incidentally, who do YOU work for?

42

Jean's Golf Clubs

WHAT FOLLOWS IS A REMARKABLE story about a lost and forgotten set of golf clubs that belonged to a dear and departed Canadian friend, Jean, how they were found, and their journey back home. It all started with a phone call late one night from a colleague and neighbor, "Ivan, are you a golfer? I have a set of golf clubs that belonged to Jean and I've kept them in my house waiting for a family member to claim them. I recently rediscovered them underneath my bed as I was packing things up to move into a new apartment."

I am not a golfer but something told me that I was meant to receive those golf clubs so I said that I would take them. At first I did not really know what I was going to do with them and for a while I even considered giving them away or selling them and donating the proceeds to a charity. Eventually it became clear that his golf clubs had landed on my lap with a purpose and that purpose was to make sure they were returned to his beloved family. Before I get into how that happened, however, here is a little background information about four individuals whose paths will be forever linked to a set of golf clubs in what started out as a casual game of golf between Jean and Mark many years ago.

I met Mark while attending Global Express (GEX) pilot initial training in February 2004 in Montreal. Mark was a superb instructor with an uncanny ability to explain something complex in a manner that made it easier for everyone to understand. In addition, Mark was simply a great guy and we hit it off right away. Despite the geographical distance between us, and the years gone by, we've been good friends ever since.

During a game of golf between Jean and Mark the subject of a job opening with Jet ExecuAir came up and Mark suggested that Jean contact me about it, and he did. Soon thereafter, I hired Jean and sent him to Challenger 601 (CL601) pilot initial training at FlightSafety International's Training Center in Montreal. Upon his return to Macao, Jean told me how impressed he was with his instructor, Lester, and that Lester might be interested in a job with Jet ExecuAir. While I was attending CL601 recurrent training a couple of months later I met Lester in person and was just as impressed as Jean had been. I promptly extended Lester an invitation for him and his wife to come to Macao for a "look-see" visit. He accepted the job, moved his family to Asia, and the rest is history. We've had a great friendship ever since. Who would have ever imagined that the start of our friendship could be traced back to a game of golf played with this lost and forgotten set of golf clubs? There is definitely a connection between all of us and those golf clubs. This is now as evident to me as the friendship we've developed over the course of several years.

With the golf clubs now sitting in a corner of my tiny Hong Kong apartment I contacted Mark, told him how I came to have them, and asked him whether he would be interested in them. He promptly said yes, but we agreed that I would contact Jean's family first to find out whether they wanted them. Jean's younger brother, Andre, was happy to hear about the golf clubs and expressed a desire to get them back. For nearly two months Andre and I had been trying to figure out how to ship Jean's golf clubs when a coworker casually mentioned that Lester was traveling to Montreal the following week on a business trip. I gave Lester a quick call and he eagerly agreed to take the golf clubs with him to Montreal and to personally hand them to Andre. The more I think about how all of this happened the more convinced I am that our dear friend Jean had a hand in ensuring that his lost and forgotten golf clubs were found, passed over to me, and then delivered to his brother Andre by our mutual friend Lester after a 7,000-mile journey from Hong Kong.

Jean may be gone, but he is definitely not forgotten. His charisma, friendly smile and sense of humor, charming French accent, love for life, and dedication to his family and friends have left an everlasting impression on those of us fortunate enough to have met him. With the return of his golf clubs to his beautiful family Jean has cleverly played one last game of golf and hit a jaw dropping 200-yard birdie straight into the 18th hole. Way to score my friend!

Mission accomplished, Jean. May you continue to enjoy clear skies, smooth air, and strong tailwinds.

43

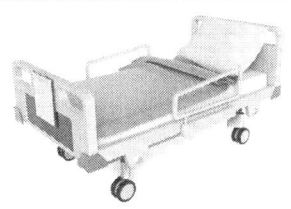

Anatomy of a bike accident

I SUFFERED A MOUNTAIN BIKING accident in October 2014 while exploring some challenging trails and technical descents with a good friend of mine. We had been having a great time on the regular trails when I decided to ask him, unwisely and in a poor display of judgment, to show me some of the more challenging trails. These new trails were narrow, winding, and engulfed by thick vegetation. Everything was going fairly well when suddenly the vegetation cleared and I was facing a short but steep and treacherous descent. I was caught completely off guard and did not, as I was supposed to, shift my body backwards to move the center of gravity aft, so when the front wheel hit a ditch I was propelled over the handlebars. In aviation speak what happened next would be described as "uncontrolled flight." I was flying, all right, but I had absolutely no control over anything. I hit the ground hard and landed on my right shoulder and torso. To add insult to injury…the bike then landed on top of me. As I lay there, face down and still slightly disoriented, I knew I was hurt but did not know where or how badly. My friend, who had been riding behind me, quickly came to my assistance and told me not to move. He promptly lifted and set the bike aside and then proceeded to check for signs of bleeding, broken bones or bruises. Other than what appeared to be a dislocated right shoulder it seemed as if I was OK. I sat down for a few minutes trying to absorb, and assess, what had just happened as well as evaluate what to do next. If my shoulder was indeed dislocated, and it sure felt that way, I would need to see a doctor. Considering that we were in an isolated area the only options to reach a nearby private clinic would be for us to either walk down the hill towards the street and then catch a taxi or, as I was inclined to do, ride our bikes slowly down a fairly easy trail and then continue riding on the street. While I was still sitting on the ground I asked my friend to use my phone to take some pictures of the accident site, including one of me…with a smile on my face in a poor attempt at disguising how I felt. To test whether I could ride I lowered the seat, sat on the bike, and grabbed the handlebars. I felt reasonably sure that if I did not put too much pressure on my right shoulder I would be able to ride the approximately 30 minutes that it would take to reach the clinic. We got going and the ride was reasonably painless but just before we reached the clinic I started to have some difficulty breathing. Luckily, we were not far from the clinic and I was able to see a doctor quickly. After the initial examination the doctor came back to discuss the results of the X-Ray tests. The news wasn't good. I did not actually have a dislocated shoulder but rather a disjointed collarbone. "You will need surgery," he said. Ouch. Not what I wanted to hear...at all. By then I started having more difficulty breathing and expressed this to him on several occasions. They eventually provided me with oxygen and a place to lie down but I still struggled to breathe. For some reason the doctor and the nurses were far more concerned with my shoulder injury than with my breathing difficulties. In my first display of good judgment that day I said to my friend, "I need to go to the hospital, now."

We left, but not before they shoved a bunch of additional bills for me to pay. We hopped in a taxi and drove straight to the Emergency section of the hospital where a Portuguese doctor promptly examined me. In a matter of minutes he concluded that my right lung had collapsed and advised that a pneumothorax procedure would be performed right away. He confirmed that the right shoulder would, indeed, require surgery but that it could wait. "We need to take care of that lung first," he said. He exuded confidence and I was glad to be there. The procedure took less than twenty minutes and consisted of inserting a drain tube into the lung cavity. Despite the local anesthesia I still felt pain as the long, thin tube went through the rib cage and into the lung cavity. However, I felt immediate relief as I heard, quite suddenly, air quickly rushing out of the tube. Trapped air in the lung cavity had collapsed the lung and prevented it from expanding. That's why I had been having so much difficulty breathing. It was still difficult to breathe but the pain and discomfort I had felt on my right torso was rapidly diminishing.

That night I called my wife, who at the time was visiting relatives in Thailand, and told her about my condition. She was by my side the following day. Her daily presence and constant encouragement gave me strength. Since I had just taken a dose of anesthesia for the pneumothorax procedure the anesthesiologist would only allow the shoulder surgery to take place three days later. Among the several visitors I received later that day was the friend I had been biking with, and his wife. They brought me some homemade cooking which was absolutely delicious. He felt terrible about the whole thing and I had to reassure him that it had been entirely my fault. I did tell him, however, that I needed a favor. After learning that my bike was OK I asked him to please take it to the shop for a full service check and to replace the rear brake pads. I also asked him to then take the bike to my apartment. He readily and happily agreed to do that. Over the next few days he continued visiting me, brought more homemade cooking, and kept me apprised of the bike's servicing status.

When I was taken into the surgery room on the third day I clearly remember seeing and hearing the nurses casually chatting as an inhaler was placed over my nose. I closed my eyes for a second or two as the nurses chatted away and when I opened them again something did not seem right. It was awfully quiet and except for a single nurse all the other nurses had suddenly vanished. Where did they go? Why had they left? Where did that shelf on the wall come from? Where is the huge and bright lamp that had been above me? What is going on? I tried to move but my arms and legs were tied down. The nurse saw me struggling and moved towards me. "When am I going to be operated on?" I managed to ask with some difficulty. To which she replied, "It's finished. You are in the recovery room." I had been gone for several hours and, thanks to the anesthesia, I had absolutely no recollection of what had happened during that time. The surgery had taken place right after I closed my eyes for what seemed like a second or two. It was surreal.

The next day I reported the bike accident and resulting surgery to my supervisor, PacificJet Airways' Manager of Flight Operations. He wished me a prompt recovery and then, as is required by the Hong Kong Civil Aviation Department (CAD), asked me to submit the corresponding unfitness report that he would then forward to the CAD. That same day I called my parents. As expected they were distraught and deeply concerned about my current condition as well as its potential impact on my aviation career. To alleviate their concerns, as well as attempt to somehow explain my passion for mountain biking, I decided to write and send them a letter. That letter, titled "Another mountain to climb," is included in this book…and eventually, and quite unexpectedly, led me to write this book.

The CAD's response arrived a few days later in the form of a letter stating that my medical certificate was "deemed to be suspended." It further stated that before I could resume flight crew duties I had to obtain a medical clearance from a CAD Authorized Medical Assessor (AMA). And so it began, the long road to full recovery, regaining my medical certificate, and returning to active flight crew status. I was facing, indeed, another challenging mountain to climb.

When I hit the ground, following my "uncontrolled flight," a rib cracked and punctured a lung. Air then slowly exited the lung and entered into the lung cavity creating a vacuum that caused the lung to collapse and prevented it from expanding. The pneumothorax procedure drained the trapped air out of the cavity and allowed the lung, over the course of several days, to gradually expand to its full size as I took deep breaths. The fall also caused a ligament, which kept the clavicle in place, to snap and cause the disjointed collarbone. The shoulder surgery replaced the damaged ligament with an artificial material made out of…polyester. When I heard about the polyester and expressed disbelief the doctor laughed and said that even the two of us trying to pull it apart at the same time would not cause it to break. I spent a total of eleven days in the hospital. For the first seven days I was restricted to the bed as the tube draining the lung cavity was still in place. It was connected to a large apparatus that collected the fluid and was attached to the bed frame. When the tube was finally removed and I was allowed to walk I had to do so slowly at first. I then spent many hours over the next few days walking around a nearby outdoor patio. I loved, and appreciated, being able to walk again with the sun and the breeze on my face. It was difficult and painful to move my arm but that did not deter me from diligently doing some simple therapy exercises the lead nurse had taught me. Before I was released from the hospital another doctor came to see me and, after moving my arm and shoulder in various directions and at different angles, stated that I would require fifteen to twenty physiotherapy sessions. During my time in the hospital the doctors and the nurses took excellent care of me. I was, and will always remain, grateful to them. Nonetheless, I couldn't wait to go home.

After the surgery I could not raise my right arm more than ninety degrees and even that resulted in considerable discomfort (translation: pain). The therapy sessions would help me raise my arm the remaining ninety degrees. So, over the next several weeks, I focused, laser-like, on my recovery. I was committed to my recovery and absolutely convinced that I would regain full shoulder mobility. I could see the future already and in that imagined future I could raise my arm fully vertical. From the moment I woke up each morning until the moment I went to sleep at night all I could think of was my recovery. The physiotherapy sessions, 2-3 times a week, were painful, and yet I found myself disappointed when the therapist would say that we were done for the day. Not only did I want to continue a bit longer but I was already eagerly anticipating the next session. In between supervised sessions I continued doing daily therapy at home. Little by little I started to see progress. To test my shoulder mobility I would sit on a chair and, pretending I was in the Gulfstream 550 cockpit, I would reach for, and try to manipulate, the various switches and knobs in the flight guidance panel as well as in the overhead panel. The overhead panel was the real challenge because I had to stretch my arm out and reach up towards all the imaginary switches and knobs...but little by little I was able to reach them all. Eventually my therapist told me that our next session together would be the last. As far as she was concerned I had already regained an acceptable level of mobility. I had only done eight sessions so far and despite my repeated pleading for more sessions she only agreed to give me one more session. After that last session the same doctor who had seen me the day I was released from the hospital examined me again and, satisfied with my shoulder mobility, pronounced me "fixed."

The next challenge would be to demonstrate to the AMA that I was indeed "fixed" and was, therefore, fit to resume flight crew duties. From the list of approved AMAs I contacted a doctor I had previously met for the renewal of my medical certificate a few years earlier. I explained via e-mail what had happened with the bike, the resulting surgery, the suspension of my medical certificate, and the progress I had made with the therapy sessions. In addition, I attached a number of medical reports, including follow-up medical reports in which the two doctors who performed the pneumothorax procedure and shoulder surgery stated that I was fully recovered and able to fly. Granted, their assessment, while greatly important to me, had absolutely no effect on lifting my medical certificate's suspension as only the AMA was qualified, and duly authorized, to perform an assessment and, if satisfied, reinstate my medical certificate. We scheduled the assessment for two weeks later, which would be five weeks since the accident. When that day arrived I was fully ready, mentally and physically, for the assessment as well as eager to be reinstated to active flight crew status. Unfortunately, it did not go well. In fact, the doctor did not even do a physical assessment. After reviewing the original medical records I had brought with me he stated that I had to wait 90 days from the date of the pneumothorax procedure before I could be assessed. That meant waiting an additional 54 days. The news nearly killed me...and not literally. As I struggled to process what I had just heard, and considered its consequences, I found myself not only in a state of shock but I couldn't breathe! The company and the Aircraft Owner had been supportive so far but I was afraid that a prolonged downtime could seriously jeopardize my job. I tried, unsuccessfully, to explain to the doctor that, as far as my job was concerned, I was only as good as my ability and just as importantly, my availability to crew the aircraft I was assigned to fly. "Come back January 17th and I'll assess you then," he said. I went home feeling deflated, demoralized, and depressed. I called my wife and from the sound of my voice she knew. Due to my current state of mind I elected to wait until the following day to break the news to PacificJet Airways, my assigned Aircraft Owner, my crew, and my parents. PacificJet Airways and the Aircraft Owner, while disappointed with the news, expressed their continued support. That support, plus the encouragement I received from family and friends, gave me a much-needed boost. Then, three or four days later, I woke up in the middle of the night with a thought. Shouldn't I get a second opinion? Why should I blindly trust this doctor? What if, after waiting for the additional 54 days to be assessed, he comes up with something else? What would happen to my job then? I made the decision right there and then that I would seek a second opinion. The following morning I contacted a senior AMA who had worked as a doctor for Cathay Pacific and, in that capacity, oversaw hundreds of airline pilots. I first spoke to him on the phone to explain my situation and we agreed that I would send him scanned copies of all the medical records so that he could review them. In the e-mail, along with the attached copies, I asked him point blank, "Is there a CAD-mandated wait period following a pneumothorax procedure before I can be assessed?" He wrote back, "There is a wait period for a spontaneous pneumothorax but that is not your case. You had a traumatic pneumothorax. I can assess you anytime." The news brought tears of joy to my eyes and gave me a much-needed morale boost. We scheduled an appointment for a week later at Cathay City's medical center while I attended recurrent simulator training at FlightSafety International, which operates a full-motion Level D, G550 flight simulator at the Cathay City training center.

I am happy to report that the shoulder performed perfectly well during the intensive simulator sessions. In addition, the AMA's assessment of my fitness went extraordinarily well. Two days later I received a letter from the CAD stating that "...any suspension of your medical certificate...is hereby lifted retrospectively" from the date of the AMA's assessment. That letter allowed me to return to active flight status right away. Later that same month I flew two trips, to Japan and Singapore, and felt absolutely...rejuvenated. Not only had I conquered that new mountain and was back flying but I was also writing about my career as an aviator. That bike accident was certainly unfortunate but out of that unfortunate event and stressful time period something positive happened: this book and perhaps even more importantly, the opportunity to share some of my experiences as a professional pilot with many others.

On a final note, when going downhill on a mountain bike don't forget to shift your body back. Doing so will keep you from going flying over the handlebar if you hit a ditch or a rock. Take my word for it. I love flying…but only when I have full control over where I am going.

44

Another mountain to climb

I WROTE THE FOLLOWING LETTER to my family after my mountain biking accident. They were very concerned about my condition and the impact the accident would have on my career. My aviation medical certificate had been temporarily suspended because of the resulting surgery. This letter is not about aviation and some people may wonder why it has been included in an aviation book. This is a story about determination, a trait every pilot must possess in order to succeed in his career. I have included it because it eventually led me to write this book.

Dear family,

Having recently injured my shoulder while riding a mountain bike I thought that it would be beneficial to explain in writing what has drawn me so passionately to this sport.

It all began one day when my wife and I were attending a BMW car exposition at The Galaxy Hotel and Casino in Macao. I have always been a fan of BMW vehicles and motorcycles and believe that nothing compares to German technology and ingenuity. "Hey Ivan, come see this bike," called my wife. Before me was a radical and sharp looking mountain bike. I must admit I did not know the first thing about mountain bikes but I knew this was love at first sight. So I said, "Start negotiating with the salesman because I am taking her home today." Despite her continued protests about the high sticker price and whether this was just a passing fad on my part, she negotiated a good deal and I became the proud owner of a BMW "Enduro" mountain bike. I don't believe in fate but having been concerned over the previous two years or so about the need to find some physical activity that I could enjoy and which would allow me to maintain my body in good physical condition, I knew instantly that this bike was the answer I had been searching for…and that's how my romance with mountain biking started.

First, I had to learn as much about the bike as possible, such as how the suspension, gears, and brakes worked and how to manipulate them; how to adjust the different bike components to fit my posture, size, and weight; and how to apply various riding techniques such as shifting my body position in order to move the center of gravity to improve rear wheel traction or to keep the front wheel from lifting during a steep ascent.

At the same time I started building up muscle strength, stamina, and endurance. My first ride barely covered a distance of five kilometers on a flat and paved terrain. Not surprisingly I was exhausted and quickly realized just how out of shape I was. However, from that point on, I started setting incremental goals for myself and eventually accomplished each and every one of them. For example, complete a 10-kilometer ride, then 15, 20, 25, and 30-kilometer rides. Next goal: complete a 20-kilometer ride in an hour or less. Needless to say I failed many times but, to a certain degree, each failure was a small victory in that with each attempt I got closer to the goal.

Since I spend a lot of time in Hong Kong I decided that I needed a second bike. So, while Maree was away on a trip, I covertly ordered a BMW "All Mountain" mountain bike. I figured that with a second bike I wouldn't find myself in HK wishing that I was in Macao just so that I could go riding. With two bikes I could now go riding regardless of whether I was in Macao or Hong Kong. Well, that stunt resulted in me being confined to the dog house for many days but, as the saying goes, sometimes "it's better to ask for forgiveness than for permission." She was very upset with me for not telling her but eventually she forgave me. Hong Kong has lots of challenging mountains and great trails and these BMW mountain bikes were designed by talented engineers to tackle these mountains and trails with ease.

So what draws me to it? Let me begin by saying that it is not a desire to do risky things – not at all. As a pilot identifying hazards and minimizing risks are ingrained into how I operate. It is not the need to find another method or activity to socialize with others. Nope. I enjoy riding and being completely alone. Just me, the bike, and the trail. It is not a desire to compete with others as a way to prove myself, gain recognition or win trophies. Nope. Each ride is indeed a competition, but I only wish to compete with myself.

My favorite part of mountain biking is to climb mountains. Having learned how to properly operate the bike and gain a fair level of physical strength and endurance, I decided to climb my first mountain. I failed miserably. Half way through the climb my legs were burning and begging for me to stop. I was out of breath and completely exhausted. On the next few attempts I did not fare any better but my resolve was undiminished. I knew that it was not a matter of "if" but rather "when" I would conquer the mountain. Despite repeated failed attempts I just kept on trying. I knew that to succeed I had to overcome two obstacles – the physical and mental barriers.

To help me a bit, I decided to employ a little reverse psychology. I named two of the mountains "You are defeated" and "Nice try, but you are still defeated," respectively. These names reflected how I felt every time I had to get off my bike and push it the rest of the way to the top: unsuccessful, exhausted, and completely out of breath. My resolve, however, never faltered. In fact I was more determined than ever to conquer these mountains. So I kept training and despite many more setbacks, I eventually reached the top. Still exhausted and out of breath but on my bike. I was elated at having made it but there was no time to waste self-congratulating. So I set myself a new goal: climb the first mountain and, without a rest break, descend and then continue on to the second mountain. Little by little I was able to eventually climb both mountains and complete the round trip without pausing or feeling too taxed.

The mountain bike is the tool and mountain biking is the activity that allows me to achieve and maintain good physical condition and mental sharpness. They are also how I satisfy my need to push and compete with myself. I love the challenge. In fact, I feel addicted to it. Failed attempts only drive me to continue on and keep trying harder.

My recent shoulder injury is a significant setback but also an opportunity for me to recognize my limitations and learn from my mistakes. I was too cocky and overconfident when I elected to deviate from my traditional type of riding and explore some highly technical and challenging descents. I won't attempt those descents again as the risks far outweigh the benefits. But I can't stop climbing mountains. I believe I can continue to do so safely. I wish the accident had never occurred, but it did. I have accepted it and its consequences. There is only one thing to do now, focus on my recovery.

While in the hospital I had a lot of time to think. For a while I contemplated whether I should continue riding or not. While lying down on my hospital bed I received a message from a friend of mine in which he, half-jokingly and half-seriously, said "Sell the bike, buy a new sofa, and enjoy life like the rest of us." He went on to say that there is "Nothing more dangerous than old guys on bikes." At 53 years of age, I am certainly not a young man but I don't consider myself old enough yet to want to swap my mountain bikes for a new sofa and embrace a sedentary lifestyle.

I will treat this injury, and the lengthy recovery process, as just another mountain to climb. As in previous occasions the outcome of this effort is not in doubt. I will recover fully and will regain my aviation medical certificate (it was automatically suspended because of the surgery). Each supervised physiotherapy session, as well as my own sessions, will help me succeed. It will take time, a great deal of effort, and many attempts, but make no mistake about it, with sheer determination on my part plus the continued support of my wife, my family and friends, I will make it to the top of this new mountain.

It is my sincere hope that the above will help alleviate your concerns about my condition as well as my passion for mountain biking. Furthermore, I hope to answer the question recently posed to me by Uncle Ignacio and which is probably shared by many of you. He asked, "What the heck were you doing on a mountain bike instead of using an ordinary Captain's chair?" Dear Uncle Ignacio, it's OK. I am fine. I just have another mountain to climb.

45

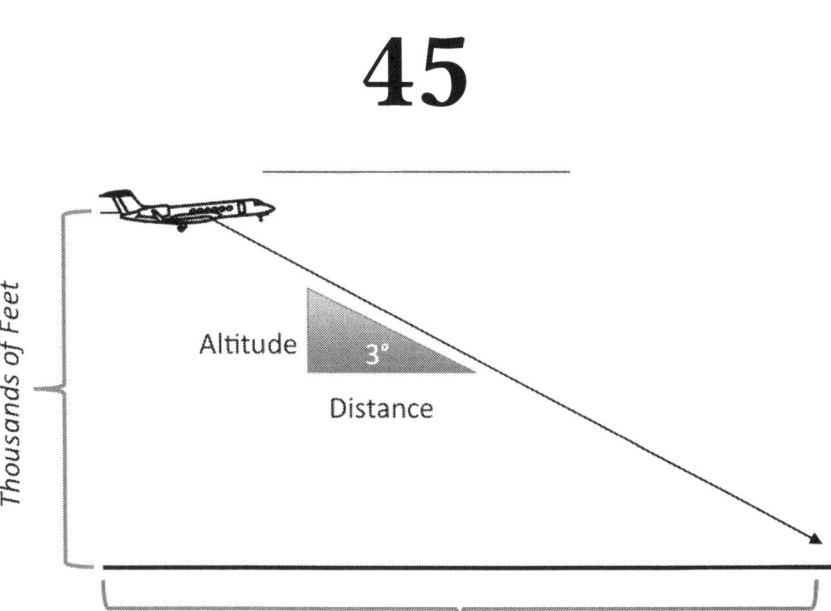

3° Top of Descent:
Start Down = Altitude (in thousands) x 3

Approaching Top of Descent point

AS OF THIS WRITING I still have eleven years remaining in my professional pilot career until I retire at 65 years old. Provided that I remain medically fit and physically able to perform my job I fully intend, and expect, to continue flying until I turn 65. Not a day later but certainly not a day earlier as I still have a lot to learn, and do. In conjunction with flying I wish to continue sharing my experience with newer generations of aviators. Eleven years may seem like a long time but I suspect they will go by in a flash. In fact I feel as if I am already approaching what could be equated with the Top of Descent (TOD) point. The TOD is an aviation term used to define a pre-calculated point along the route in which the aircraft transitions from the cruise phase of flight to the descent phase. The latter is then followed by an approach and landing at the airport. Once you arrive at the destination, the trip, or journey, is then over. As I get closer to my career's TOD point I can't help but feel that I have already climbed as high as I can, and aspired to, and that the time to start preparing psychologically for an eventual descent and landing is near. So the question is, what do I hope to do, or better yet, what do I expect to accomplish by the time I perform that last approach and landing at my home base in March 2026, and I have to hang up my wings?

As in every journey, there is always a beginning…and eventually an ending. For me the journey began when I saw the U.S. Air Force Thunderbirds performing at an air show when I was a young kid. Remarkably for someone that young I decided, right there and then, that I would become an aviator someday and fly jets. Setting up such an ambitious goal at that early age was clearly a defining moment in my life. But a goal, like any journey, is much more than simply deciding on a destination. It's what you do on the way to your destination, and just as importantly, how you do it, that makes a difference. As a professional pilot whose career currently spans 34 years I have been quite fortunate to have accomplished everything I set out to do…and a lot more.

Don't get me wrong though. It has not been an easy journey by any means. As can be expected in any career path there have been ups and downs along the way and, often, there were more downs than ups. In fact, I clearly recall some moments filled with uncertainty and even anxiety. However, thanks to a fervent desire and focused determination to become an aviator, an obstinate perseverance in the face of obstacles, an unrelenting, if not obsessive, desire to excel in my chosen career, plus a considerable dose of good luck, I was able to endure long enough to reach each and every one of my objectives. Overall it can be said that it has been a satisfying and rewarding journey and I am optimistic it will continue to be so over the next eleven years.

Despite the considerable challenges typically encountered in an aviation career I am grateful to have achieved some significant milestones. These include: graduating from Metropolitan State College with a Bachelor's degree in Aerospace Science, completing basic and advanced flight training, obtaining initial pilot certification and ratings, working as a Flight Instructor, accumulating and reaching the first 1,000 flight hours, and choosing to pursue and to focus on a career as a corporate pilot. The next stage consisted of getting my first decent job, transitioning to turboprop and then to turbojet aircraft, upgrading to Captain, mastering new aircraft types, and becoming an experienced international jet pilot. This was followed by becoming a Training Captain and pilot examiner, becoming a manager and eventually reaching a Director level position. Other milestones included, obtaining pilot license certification from six countries, successfully completing several hundred training courses, setting up a flight department, being admitted by Embry-Riddle Aeronautical University and obtaining a Master's degree and a Corporate Aviation Management Program (CAMP) certificate, and reaching and surpassing the 10,000 flight-hour mark. More recently... writing a book in the hope of motivating and inspiring others to pursue and achieve their own dreams. Although I have now slowed down the pace considerably there are still a lot of things I want to do in my remaining years as a professional pilot, like mastering the Gulfstream 550 and, hopefully, the newer fly-by-wire Gulfstream 650.

Eventually I will arrive at the end of the journey and what better way to reach that point than to continue flying safely. So that's primarily what I expect to do, and accomplish, in the next eleven years: complete my aviation career, this remarkable journey, safely, and then begin the next journey, retirement. Incidentally, I have never been a golfer or enjoyed fishing and have absolutely no desire to start, or spend, my retirement journey swinging clumsily at a little ball or catching fish. Instead, I may just write another book or two while traveling around the world with my soulmate and companion, my lovely wife Maree.

It is still a long way to go but I can already visualize what my last flight as a professional pilot will hopefully look like. Following a smooth landing after an uneventful flight, I can see myself vacating the runway, then taxiing slowly to the ramp and going underneath the pre-arranged and traditional water gun salute (high pressure water jet streams arching upwards from the nozzles of two fire trucks positioned on opposite sides of the ramp) in recognition of my last flight. Then, following the marshaller's signals to bring the aircraft to a gentle stop at the parking stand, I will shut the engines down, get out of my seat for the last time, open the main cabin door, shake hands with my crew and passengers, and express my heartfelt gratitude to my crew for their support over the years. Finally, as I slowly walk away, my dream and journey as an aviator fully realized and completed, I will be mentally prepared to commence the next chapter in my personal life, and will do so with the same level of determination and focus as that young kid who watched an airshow so many years ago.

Thank you for reading my book. If you enjoyed it, won't you please take a moment to leave me a review at your favorite online retailer? Good luck as you pursue your dreams and embark on your own journey. Happy landings!

Ivan Luciani

ABOUT THE AUTHOR

IVAN LUCIANI IS A CORPORATE PILOT who has logged over 10,000 flight hours flying around the world, and whose aviation career currently spans 34 years. He has flown private and public transport operations in a variety of business jets, including the Bombardier Global Express and, more recently, the Gulfstream 450 and 550. In addition to being a Captain he has also held several managerial posts. While he may be an experienced pilot, he readily and openly admits that, he is definitely an amateur author. Ivan lives in Hong Kong and in Macao with his Thai wife.

CONNECT WITH IVAN LUCIANI

Connect with me on LinkedIn:

hk.linkedin.com/pub/ivan-luciani/4/2a0/680

Follow me on Twitter:

@iluciani2002

Follow me on Instagram:

iluciani

Send feedback via e-mail:

myaviationjourney@gmail.com

Made in the USA
Lexington, KY
20 September 2016